BASIC ILLUSTRATED

Sea Kayaking

Revised Edition

Roger Schumann

FALCON GUIDES

GUILFORD, CONNECTICUT
HELENA, MONTANA

FALCONGUIDES®

An imprint of Rowman & Littlefield
Falcon and FalconGuides are registered trademarks and Make Adventure Your Story is a
trademark of Rowman & Littlefield.

Distributed by NATIONAL BOOK NETWORK

British Library Cataloguing in Publication Information Available

Library of Congress Cataloging in Publication Data

Names: Schumann, Roger.
Title: Basic illustrated sea kayaking / Roger Schumann.
Description: Revised Edition. | Guilford, Connecticut : FalconGuides, [2016]
   | "Distributed by NATIONAL BOOK NETWORK"—T.p. verso. | Includes index.
Identifiers: LCCN 2015048554 (print) | LCCN 2015050602 (ebook) | ISBN
   9781493016518 (paperback : alk. paper) | ISBN 9781493024582 (e-book)
Subjects: LCSH: Sea kayaking.
Classification: LCC GV788.5 .S37 2016 (print) | LCC GV788.5 (ebook) | DDC
   797.122/4—dc23
LC record available at http://lccn.loc.gov/2015048554

∞™ The paper used in this publication meets the minimum requirements of American National
Standard for Information Sciences—Permanence of Paper for Printed Library Materials, ANSI/NISO
Z39.48-1992.

Contents

Introduction

Sleek and full of promise, there's something inherently alluring about a sea kayak. Even the shyest of toddlers waddling down the beach will stop and stare before venturing closer, drawn to the cockpit like the needle of a compass to north. She'll look back at her parents, eyes hopeful, wordlessly begging the question: *Can I sit in it, pleeease?* The parents may translate the question aloud but will be too shy to ask for themselves. But you can often see their own desire in their eyes as well.

Fiordo Comau, Patagonia, Chile KIM GRANDFIELD

Sea kayaks move people, both physically and literally, like some sort of visual pheromone. But it goes beyond the visual. If you listen closely to a sea kayak at rest on the beach, it's not hard to imagine the howl of an arctic wolf or the wind.

Or not.

Sea kayaks are also accessible, versatile, accommodating—as adventurous or tame as you care to get. They're as well suited for a for a weeks-long expedition down Alaska's Inside Passage or a Patagonian fiord as they are for a trip to the local lake for an early morning of floating and fishing, a lazy summer afternoon at the beach with the kids, or an evening workout to clear your head after a hard day's work.

A sea kayak is sleeker and more seaworthy than a canoe, easier to launch than a motorboat, and so user-friendly that most people will need little or no instruction to operate one—at least not until they tip over, which at some point is virtually inevitable, and where having a little knowledge can be convenient at least and could save a life at best.

This book, among other things like gear and paddling skills, will cover safety and introduce trip planning strategies to help you avoid potentially dangerous situations. The "Getting Started" sections in each chapter focus on the basics. The "Getting Serious" sections include more advanced skills for those ready to go beyond the basics. Either way, seek competent instruction along your learning journey. No matter how well written, books are supplemental information and not intended to replace on-water training sessions.

The more skills you gain, the farther afield you can explore. Kayaks in skilled hands are amazingly seaworthy and can take you pretty much anywhere you want to go. People in kayaks have crossed the Atlantic, more than once; crossed the Pacific from Monterey Bay, California, to Maui; circumnavigated Australia, twice; and completed a three-year rounding of South America. For most of us, our goals will likely be less ambitious than crossing oceans and circling continents—to simply catch a whiff of salt-sea air on the weekend, catch a fish, or catch a few easy waves after work will be enough to justify the time and effort it takes to build our skills to a comfortable level— but the potential is there. Waiting. Just beyond the next bend in the shoreline, just over the horizon.

Section I:
Boats and Gear

Watching fin whales, Bahia de Los Angeles, Baja California, Mexico Roger Schumann

Traditional skin-on-frame hunting kayak HELEN WILSON, GREENLANDORBUST.COM

CHAPTER ONE

Sea Kayaks and Sea Kayakers

A kayak without a kayaker, it's been said, is like a body without a soul. It requires a partner to animate it and transform both of you. When slipping into their sealskin kayaks, ancient kayak hunters from maritime cultures considered themselves able to shape-shift into marine mammals—on even footing with the ones they set out to catch.

If hunting seals to survive, you needed a long, narrow kayak that was sleek and stealthy, efficient and seaworthy for covering long miles at sea. Inland cultures hunting caribou at river crossings used shorter, wider kayaks that didn't need to be efficient just to paddle a couple hundred meters from shore, just stable and maneuverable enough to dart around a heard of thrashing caribou. As a modern kayaker, you'll need to decide what you're hunting—be it a little solitude or a big adventure, a little exercise or a big fish—and choose a kayak (or kayaks) that's best suited.

The long and short of it Peter Donohue

Types of Kayakers: What Level Paddler Do You Want to Be?

Give some thought to the type of kayaker you are now and the one you want to become so that you don't end up trying to hunt seals on the open sea in a boat better suited for caribou. Also consider the necessary skill set implied with where you want to go.

For talking about skill levels or the relative difficulty of sea conditions you feel comfortable paddling in, it's helpful to have a scale such as the one snow skiers use, with ratings like black diamonds and blue squares. A bit less colorful, the Level 1 through Level 5 scale on the facing page is based on the one the American Canoe Association uses. One of the largest paddlesports organizations in the world, the ACA provides safety and skills education to recreational paddlers and certification for instructors in canoeing, rafting, stand up paddle boarding (SUP), and kayaking. The scale considers both how rough the water conditions are and distance from shelter. Any terms you don't yet know will be explained in subsequent chapters; for now, "knots" can be substituted with "miles per hour."

As with any system, lines drawn are somewhat arbitrary, and kayakers may not fit neatly into boxes. Nonetheless, it's a good starting point for getting a sense of the sorts of challenges presented at each level. Below is some elaboration on the skill levels.

Bahia Magdalena, Baja California, Mexico ROGER SCHUMANN

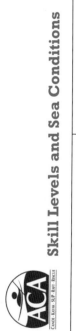

CANOE KAYAK SUP RAFT RESCUE

Skill Levels and Sea Conditions

	Getting Started	Getting Serious			
	L1: Introduction to Flat Water	L2: Calm-Water Touring	L3: Basic Kayak Touring	L4: Open Water Touring	L5: Advanced Open Water
Sea conditions, wind, waves	Flat water, light breeze	Light chop, wind < 10 kts	Wind to 10 kts, white-caps, waves to 1'	Wind 10–15 kts; waves and seas 1'–3'	Wind 15–25+ kts; waves/seas: 3'–5'+
Exposure	Easy swimming distance to shore	Well within 0.5 mile of shore in protected areas with numerous easy landing beaches	Up to 0.5 mile from shore or nearest beach, including open-water crossings of up to 1 mile	Up to 1 mile from shore or nearest beach, including open-water crossings of up to 2 miles	Exposed, challenging shorelines beyond 1 mile from shore or nearest beach, crossings > 2 miles
Currents	None	<1 kt	<2 kts	2–3 kts	3–6+ kts
Surf	None	None	To 1'	1'–3'	3'–5'+
Navigational Skills	None	Basic piloting	Basic chart reading and compass use	Comfortable using chart and compass in combination with tidal-current information	Complex navigation skills
Kayak	Any	Any with enough flotation for deepwater rescue	Touring kayak or sit-on-top	Touring kayak or sit-on-top	Touring kayak

Level 1 paddlers are just getting started or plan to paddle in calm, protected areas, such as small lakes and marinas with little boat traffic, paddling near the beach or dock you launched from as opposed to actually going anywhere or "touring." If the wind begins blowing, you plan to head for shore. You haven't learned deepwater rescues yet, so your safety depends on staying within easy swimming distance of easily accessible shorelines.

Level 2 paddlers still plan to stay in relatively calm conditions but have the skills and knowledge to begin venturing beyond swimming distance from shore and may actually go somewhere—albeit along a shoreline with many easy landing options, allowing you to get off the water quickly if necessary. You can handle a little wind (if blowing from a "safe" direction) and choppy water, but if whitecaps start to form, you plan to head for protection. You're capable and comfortable performing deepwater self- and assisted rescues in relatively calm water.

At **Level 3** you're ready to plan longer, more committing journeys and paddling up to 0.5 mile from shore or the nearest landing beach, including crossings of bays or to islands of up to 1 mile (never farther than 0.5 mile from either shore). You're comfortable paddling and performing rescues in L3 conditions.

Levels 4 and 5 paddlers enjoy more exposed conditions and paddling in rougher seas and are prepared to roam a mile or more from shore or between accessible beaches. You're comfortable paddling and performing rescues and rolls in L4 or L5 conditions, including currents and surf, and you can do complex on-water navigation.

Pigeon Point Lighthouse KIM GRANDFIELD

Getting Started: Choosing a Kayak

The term "sea" kayak is a bit of a misnomer, as kayaks float on both fresh and salt water and are as common on lakes and rivers as they are on the sea. *Touring* kayak is probably a more specific term, meaning a longish kayak designed to track well in a straight line, cover distance, and carry some gear.

For the original kayakers, selecting a kayak was simple—whatever the village boat builder made for you. Sea hunting kayaks were custom fit, typically three arm spans long, made of driftwood frames covered with sealskin. They were fast but narrow and tippy, so you developed the skills necessary from childhood to keep them upright and to roll them back upright when you did capsize—rescue training was essentially a matter of roll or drown.

Recreational Touring, Touring, Sit-on-Top, Whitewater PETER DONOHUE

Nowadays the vast array of choices in design, materials, and features can be dizzying—from a tubby 8-foot $400 plastic recreational kayak to an 18-foot carbon-fiber speedster costing well over 4 grand. For tootling along shore, just about anything will do; but if you want to venture farther afield, you'll want something seaworthy and efficient.

You might consider a double (or *tandem*) kayak if you're planning to paddle with kids or if one partner is much stronger than the other. However, two single kayaks are more versatile, and you can tow slower partners using a towline, essentially turning two singles into a tandem. Couples should bear in mind that doubles are sometimes called "divorce boats," so try some double dates before committing to anything long term.

Types of Kayaks: Getting Started with the Long and Short of It

Two main categories to choose between are touring and recreational kayaks, but the lines become blurred where they meet (recreational touring kayak?). Length and width are the most obvious characteristics that affect performance. In general, longer and narrower means faster but tippier and harder to turn; shorter is slower but more maneuverable; wider is slower but more stable. But manufacturers tweak hull designs to make longer kayaks more maneuverable or shorter kayaks faster, so the only way to know for sure is to paddle them.

Check your kayak's flotation before paddling beyond swimming distance from shore.
PETER DONOHUE

Types of Kayaks

	Length	Width	Flotation—Rescue	Edging Ability	Purpose/Skill Level
Touring	14'−18'+	20"−26"	Yes	Yes	Multipurpose/L1−5
Recreational	<14'	26"−30"+	No	No	Limited/L1
Touring/Rec Hybrids	10'−15'	24"−30"+	Depends	Depends	Depends
Sit-on-Tops	9'−18'+	>20"−34"+	Yes	Usually no	Depends

Two important characteristics to consider in regards to how serious you want to get are *flotation* and *edging ability*. Flotation refers to how much buoyancy a kayak has when swamped, and whether there's enough to perform deepwater rescues. Touring designs typically have waterproof compartments in the *bow* and *stern* (front and back) with enough flotation to allow you to climb back aboard and pump out the water after a capsize. Without adequate flotation, the boat might not sink, but the cockpit will flood when you try to get back in.

Check flotation in shallow water, just in case. PETER DONOHUE

Edge-ability is related to performance. The *primary stability* (resistance to tipping) of a wide, stable rec boat may feel comforting at first, but if you aspire to *push your edges* both figuratively and literally, you'll want a kayak designed to do so. When edged slightly, more performance-oriented kayaks tend to lock in to their *secondary stability* and become more maneuverable, actually carving turns like a snow ski. These kayaks generally have thigh braces that give more edging control for advanced maneuvers like bracing and rolling.

Touring Kayaks

Pros: Long and sleek, touring kayaks are the versatile, go-anywhere SUVs of the fleet. Averaging in the 16- to 17-foot range, their length helps them cover the miles efficiently. By choosing a model on the more stable end of the spectrum, even a total beginner should feel comfortable paddling one within a few minutes. Waterproof hatches in front and back provide flotation for deep-water rescues and room to store safety and camping gear. Appropriate for L1–L5, touring kayaks may be overkill for L1 or fishing.

Cons: Price, but you get what you pay for in increased performance and seaworthiness. To paddle touring kayaks safely, training in capsize-recovery techniques is required.

Recreational Kayaks

Pros: Inexpensive, stable, and user-friendly, generally with large, open cockpits that are easy to climb in and out of—more like a canoe (or a bathtub) than a traditional sea kayak—making them popular for flat-water fishing near shore.

Cons: Performance and versatility are on the low end of the spectrum, and their large, open cockpits flood easily. Lacking flotation for deepwater rescues makes them generally unsafe for paddling beyond L1 conditions.

Recreational/Touring Hybrids

Pros/Cons: When you start crossing touring and rec kayaks, it just depends on which traits end up receiving the recessive gene, especially the ones controlling flotation and edging. There are stable, inexpensive rec-style touring kayaks with enough flotation to do deepwater rescues, but without thigh braces or edging ability. A kayak like this might lack performance but still be safe enough to paddle in L2 or L3 conditions.

Sit-on-Tops

Pros: Typical sit-on-tops are stable and user-friendly, like rec boats, but more seaworthy since there's no cockpit to flood. If you fall off, you just climb back on, making them a safer option for getting beyond L1 for paddlers without rescue skills. Ideal for fishing.

Cons: Because of a higher center of gravity, SOTs need to be wider than sit-insides to achieve the same level of stability. Wider equals slower; no cockpit means no thigh braces, no edging, and less performance.

Materials and Construction

Along with the style of kayak, what it's made of affects performance, durability, weight, and cost. Today the most common choices are plastic (molded polyethylene) and glass (fiberglass or composite), along with a handful of other materials.

Plastic

Since their introduction in the 1980s (when *real* sea kayaks were made of fiberglass), plastic kayaks have come to dominate the market. No longer the cheap, overweight ugly ducklings of the fleet, polyethylene sea kayaks now come in numerous sleek, high-performance designs—in addition to the innumerable low-end varieties currently flooding the market.

They typically weigh a few pounds more than their composite cousins, but they're more durable. On the water, the differences in the weight and performance of similar designs in plastic and composite will likely be slight enough that many paddlers can't tell much difference.

Although resistant to impact, plastic takes some care in transport and storage. Plastic can warp, and nothing kills the performance of a plastic hull like big dents where you left it in the hot sun on your car rack without proper support. Also, all plastics are not created equal: Some manufacturers cut weight by making their kayaks thinner. A heavier, stiffer kayak is more resistant to warping and will outperform a light, thin one.

Composite

Kayaks made of molded fiberglass-and-resin composite remain at the crest of the wave in terms of quality. Price be damned, the performance of their stiff, smooth, lightweight hulls is unparalleled, though not indestructible. While relatively durable, more care is required compared to plastic to not crack a hull if you smack into a rock or drop one off your car, but repairs aren't too difficult. If you're willing to spend more, top-of-the-line versions built with carbon fiber or Kevlar are even lighter.

Skin-on-Frame

A small but enthusiastic number of paddlers are returning to their roots with traditional skin-on-frame (SOF) kayaks. Durable, waterproof fabrics replace sealskin in most cases, and wooden frames are sometimes exchanged for aluminum, but the look and feel of these kayaks is timeless. Performance is similar to a hard-shell, but SOFs move with the water as you paddle and are said to "feel alive." Custom-built works of art, just like the old days, SOFs' cost and durability are similar to composites, but their weight is even less.

Wood

Wood provides an art-project option for DIYers. Boats, kits, and plans are readily available in a limited number of designs, from basic plywood versions to intricate wood-strip beauties. Performance, weight, and durability are similar to composite. Cost of a kit can be less than half of a pre-built kayak—until you calculate your labor.

Portable: Folding Kayaks and Inflatables

A few manufacturers offer skin-on-frame folding kayaks, "boats in a backpack," allowing travelers to check a kayak with their bags and reassemble it at their destinations. Although some handle reasonably well, their focus tends more toward portability than performance. Inflatable kayaks are mostly inexpensive recreational models lacking performance, but being filled with air makes them inherently more seaworthy than plastic rec boats.

Kayak Features

Like cars, kayaks include a variety of features to consider. Sunroofs come standard, as do seats; but as with cars, not all seats are created equal.

Outfitting: Seats, Foot and Thigh Braces

Outfitting refers to things like the seat and foot braces that make your kayak fit better and be more comfortable. Performance-oriented designs include thigh braces and hip pads, which are often adjustable. The more snugly your kayak fits, the more control you have—to a point.

Hatches, Bulkheads, Flotation

Hatches allow access to gear stowed in the "waterproof" compartments. "Water resistant" is more realistic, since compartments generally leak a little, either through the hatch covers or through the *bulkheads* (dividers that

Anatomy of a kayak PETER DONOHUE

separate the cockpit from the compartments). Since leaky compartments can compromise flotation and safety, it's wise to test them periodically. Rescue practice is the best way to do this. A cup to a quart in your compartment isn't bad. A gallon or more is unsafe and should be fixed.

Touring kayaks typically have a compartment in the bow and stern.

Rec boats often have no hatches or have small compartments that don't provide much flotation. Boats without compartments can sometimes be made more seaworthy by stuffing a float bag (large, inflatable, boat-shaped) into the bow and/or stern.

Rudders and Skegs

Both rudders and skegs are used to help a kayak track in a straight line, and rudders are also used for steering. Rudders can be nice for long-distance touring and for photography, since they allow you to steer with your feet while you focus on paddling or taking photos. Smaller, stationary *skegs*, which help with tracking but don't steer, tend to be preferred for performance paddling because boats with the rudder down don't maneuver as quickly, and with the rudder up they often have a loose feel to the foot braces, since most need to move in order to steer.

Rudder (yellow kayak) vs. skeg (orange) PETER DONOHUE

Deck Lines

Deck or perimeter lines on most touring kayaks run along the edges of the deck. They give you something to grab a hold of, especially during rescues.

Ready to Buy: Getting Serious

With all the choices in designs, materials, and features, the best way to figure out what will work best for you is to paddle a variety of kayaks before buying. Take a class or two to build your skills so that you'll have a better idea of what you want. Some kayak shops offer demo days where you can compare a wide range of types side by side, kind of like speed dating. As you narrow your choices, you may be able to rent a few different boats for the day to get to know them better—and have the shop apply your rental fees to an eventual purchase. Try deepwater rescues to test the flotation and to see if the hatches leak. Realize that every kayak is a compromise, so look for a *good* fit rather than letting yourself get too hung up on finding the *perfect* fit.

CHAPTER TWO

Gear

It's not unusual to spend nearly as much for all the gear that goes along with kayaking as for your kayak. Although there is specific "safety gear" like emergency flares and first-aid kits, *most* gear is related to safety: Your paddle moves you away from hazards, and proper clothing keeps you from becoming dangerously hypothermic.

In head: weather report, tide times, knowledge, etc.

In pockets: knife, rescue flares, radio, compass, snack bars, etc.

Spare paddle

Spray skirt

Whistle

Paddle

In hatches: first-aid and repair kits, spare warm clothes, etc.

Paddle float

Kayaking gear PETER DONOHUE

Getting Started: Dressing for Success

Because the biggest threat to sea kayakers statistically is hypothermia (leading to drowning), the oft-repeated maxim "Dress for immersion" implies choosing your outfit based on the temperature of the water rather than the air. You can become hypothermic—to the point of losing muscular and mental functioning—with an extended immersion in water as warm as 70°F.

To avoid this, dress in layers of synthetic wicking fabrics—fleece, wool, or neoprene that keep you warm even when wet—covered by a wind- and water-resistant outer shell. "Cotton kills" is a common saying among outdoor professionals, referring to cotton's chilling effect once it gets wet, although this makes it a good choice for warm-water paddling.

Dressing safely can be particularly challenging on warm days in cold water, but the thinking is that it's easier to *cool off* when surrounded by cold

Left to right: wetsuit with paddling jacket, farmer john/jane wetsuit, dry suit Peter Donohue

water than *to warm yourself back up* after becoming chilled. Splash yourself in the face, remove a layer, or practice rescue skills, which helps you learn how many layers you really need to stay warm.

Dressing for Immersion: Getting Serious

For more ambitious trips in cold water and for rescue practice, kayakers commonly wear wetsuits or dry suits.

Wetsuits and Paddling Jackets

The extra range of motion of an armless, 3 mm "farmer john" wetsuit with a paddling-jacket shell makes it a popular choice, typically worn over a long-sleeved fleece shirt. Short-legged wetsuits or neoprene shorts are common in warmer waters. A windbreaker works as a shell, but paddling jackets sport snug-fitting neoprene closures at the wrists and neck to help keep water out. *Dry tops* are paddling jackets with latex gaskets at wrist and neck openings, making them virtually waterproof.

Dry Suits

Dry suits are like dry tops for your entire body. Instead of stopping at your waist, the jacket continues to your feet, like one-piece footie pajamas, so only your head and hands get wet. Although costing as much as some kayaks, dry suits are your safest option, and they have become increasingly popular as paddlers realize that owning one helps them improve faster. Building skills often involves falling in the water, and wearing a dry suit reduces the prospect of getting wet and cold. "It's changed the way I paddle" is a frequent refrain of new dry suit owners. Be aware that neck gaskets rub some people the wrong way, causing chafing and ripping out at inopportune times if they aren't maintained properly and replaced regularly.

If you decide to invest in a dry suit, it doesn't pay to scrimp on features. Pay extra for breathable fabric to minimize the clamminess quotient and a relief zipper so that you don't have to strip down every time you need to pee. Spring for the *overskirt* that covers your spray skirt tunnel, reducing the water entering your cockpit if you paddle in rough water or practice rolling.

Spare Warm Clothes in a Dry Bag

Whether they are damp from falling in the water or simply from sweating, paddlers often get chilled during lunch breaks. Changing out of a damp shirt will increase your comfort and could prevent you (or a partner) from becoming hypothermic. Pack an extra fleece top, windbreaker, and fleece beanie in a waterproof dry bag in case of emergency or simply to change into at lunch.

Life Vest

Like wearing your seatbelt in your car, wearing your life vest (also called a *personal flotation device,* or *PFD*) is statistically the single biggest thing you can do to increase your safety. Every year statistics show that about 90 percent of those who drown in boating accidents are not wearing life vests. While the Coast Guard does require that all kayakers *carry* approved PFDs on their boats, it stops short of requiring adults to actually wear them. People think they'll be able to put on a PFD if they need it, but after having fallen in the water, most people who've survived to tell the tale found this next to impossible.

The national *WEAR IT!* campaign educates boaters how to wear PFDs correctly: fastened snuggly enough not to float off over your head when you hit the water. Coast Guard–approved Type III vests (marked on the inside label) are designed specifically for kayaking. Spending a bit more for one that's sleek and comfortable will make you more likely to wear it. If it has pockets to stash handy items like sunscreen, snack bars, whistle (also required), and compass, it'll be convenient as well.

Footwear

Foot protection is great if you need to land on a rocky beach. Choose something that will stay on your feet if you swim but isn't too heavy to swim in.

Neoprene booties are the classic choice, but high-tech water shoes are gaining in popularity.

Paddle

After your kayak, your choice of paddle will most affect the type of paddler you want to be, as well as your comfort and enjoyment. Since you'll average some 1,000 strokes per mile and 3,000 per hour, a heavy, poorly sized paddle can take some fun out of paddling and retard skill development. Don't scrimp. This is one place where you'll get the most bang for your buck.

Left to right: Stick, low-angle touring Euro, hi-angle Euro, racing wing PETER DONOHUE

Styles of Paddles and Paddlers: Getting Started

Low-angle Paddling Style
Low-angle style refers to holding the paddle in a more horizontal position during your forward stroke, with hands around mid-chest, which feels more natural and easier on your arms. While this more relaxed stroke has higher MPG ratings than a more vertical style, it's less conducive to advanced maneuvers,

Paddle Features

Three Basic Styles: The spoon-shaped "Euro-blade"—what many consider "typical"—is most common. Another popular choice is narrow, traditional-style paddles (aka "skinny sticks"); while there are various styles, such as Aleut, Greenland paddles (GPs) are the most common sticks. A wing is a Euro-style with an extra scoop used primarily for racing.

Paddle Length: Typically measured in centimeters, ranging from 200 to 260 cm. Longer is necessary for wider kayaks; length gives more leverage but quickly becomes unwieldy, especially for linking advanced, maneuvering strokes.

Blade Width: As narrow as 3 inches for GPs, and 4–8 inches for Euro-blades. Narrower is like low gear in your car and easier on your arms. Wider is more powerful, but takes more muscle to power it. Somewhere in between is "just right" for most paddlers.

Blade Length: Longer blades tend to be narrower and used with a "low-angle" style; shorter tend to be wider for a "high-angle" style (see below).

Materials, Cost, and Weight: From heavy, cheap aluminum shafts with plastic blades, to midrange fiberglass blades and shafts, to pricey lightweight carbon-fiber blades and shafts, along with various combinations. Wood remains popular as a specialty material.

Blade Shape: Any sea kayak paddle worth its salt has asymmetrical blades (the upper lobe being longer) that are spoon-shaped with a definite face and back. Only the cheapest of the cheap are symmetrical—unless they're GPs.

One-piece and Take-apart: Most paddles are two-piece take-apart types (the shaft comes apart in the middle), making them more convenient for storage and transport, as well for carrying on deck as a spare. The ferrule joining halves typically allows some adjustment of feather angle (see below) and sometimes length. One-piece paddles are slightly lighter and stronger (ferrules add weight and a weak spot) but less convenient to store and transport.

Feather Angle: When the blades are in the same plane, the paddle is "unfeathered" or has a 0-degree feather angle. With feathered paddles, the plane of the blades is offset. Basic ferrules on take-apart paddles commonly give two options: 0 degree and either 60 degrees or 45 degrees, while fully adjustable ferrules allow any angle. When paddling into a headwind, a feathered paddle's out-of-water blade slices through the wind rather than pushing perpendicularly against it. As feather angles drop below 60 degrees, however, this becomes less of an advantage. The disadvantages are having to adjust your grip to get the feathered blade into the water at the right angle for strokes and braces and that they tend to catch in a side wind.

Bent Shaft and Smaller Diameter: If you grip a paddle tightly, your wrists will be bent slightly. Adding a bend in the shaft where it's held allows for a tight grip with a straight wrist. Since this can also be accomplished with a more-relaxed grip, you'll have to decide whether it's worth the extra cost and losing the flexibility to change hand position. For smaller hands, some manufacturers offer smaller-diameter shafts.

although it is popular with long-distance expedition paddlers. Low-angle paddles are longer overall, with longer, narrower blades.

Suggestions: A typical low-angle length is 220–230 cm for touring kayaks less than 25 inches wide. Wider kayaks, sit-on-tops, or doubles require lengths in the 230–240 cm range, up to 260 cm for extra-wide sit-on-top doubles.

High-angle Paddling Style
Popularized by racers and whitewater kayakers, a *high-angle* style is the current trend among performance-oriented sea kayakers. Paddle length tends

Low-angle and high-angle paddling styles PETER DONOHUE

to be shorter overall, with shorter, wider blades. Held at a higher, more vertical angle with hands around face height, shorter paddles are easier to plant closer to the side of the kayak—making them more effective for the high-cadence stroke used for sprinting, for vertical maneuvering strokes, and for moving quickly from side to side during the sudden braces and maneuvers required in waves, tidal races, and rock gardens. When touring, a relaxed, low-angle stroke can still be used with a high-angle paddle.

Suggestions: Lengths range from 200 to 220 cm, with 205–215 cm being the most common for touring kayaks around 24 inches wide or less. Manufacturers offer both full-width (around 8 inches) and mid-width (7 inches) blades, which all but the burliest of paddlers find more than adequate.

Traditional Paddling Style

Skinny sticks help develop a better feel for the blade and are a superior tool for working on various rolling techniques. More conducive to a low-angle style, in skilled hands they can be used in rough-water situations. However, it's more challenging to bury as much of the long blades as quickly as a shorter, wider paddle to get the same amount of surface area for vertical maneuvering strokes.

Suggestions: Length for sticks is traditionally measured at one arm span plus the distance from elbow to fingertips.

Styles of Paddles and Paddlers: Getting Serious

The best paddlers are fluent with a variety of paddles and styles from skinny stick to racing wing. The blade finesse for rolling with a skinny stick along with traditional techniques like extended-paddle positions and sliding stroke all translate well to fat blades to help you become more versatile. Similarly, using a wing refines your forward sprinting efficiency, and switching to a low-angle stroke during a long day gives weary arms a welcome break.

Other Gear

- **Spare Paddle:** Like having a spare tire, carrying a spare paddle is standard practice in case your primary paddle breaks or gets lost.

- **Spray Skirt:** Spray skirts seal off the cockpit after you sit in it, making it seaworthy. It's what makes a kayak a kayak instead of just a skinny canoe. It keeps water from dripping in your lap in calm seas and from flooding the cockpit when it gets rough. Novices might forgo the skirt if sticking to L1 conditions, or they might prefer a

Greenlandic paddler using a traditional "stick." HELEN WILSON

nylon skirt that fits loosely around the cockpit and falls off easily. But anyone planning to get serious will want a snug-fitting neoprene skirt that clings tightly to the cockpit during advanced techniques like edging or rolling.

- **Hats and Helmets:** Sunhats are good for preventing sunburn; fleece, wool, or neoprene beanies for warmth; helmets for saving your noggin when launching and landing in surf or around rocks. Helmets designed for kayaking use hardware and glues that won't corrode in water.

- **Dry Bags:** Hatches leak, so stow gear in waterproof dry bags. Several smaller bags are more versatile and easier to stow than one or two large ones.

- **First-Aid and Repair Kits:** For common injuries and gear repairs on the water, first-aid and repair kits should be waterproof and accessible. Electrical or duct tape can be handy for quick temporary repairs of boats or bodies. A compact multi-tool and repair materials kit (spare nuts and bolts, wire, etc.) are also useful.

- **Food and Water:** Snack bars in a PFD pocket are great for quick energy, and a handy water bottle or hands-free hydration pack helps you stay hydrated.

- **Bilge Pump and Sponge:** A handheld pump is essential for removing water from your cockpit after a capsize, so keep it secure but accessible.

- **Paddle Float Self-Rescue Device:** Useful for many things besides rescues—extra flotation in a leaky hatch, an air splint for limb injuries, and to help someone being towed to stabilize himself (see Rescue chapter 8). Get one with two air chambers (which can still be used if one springs a leak) or a non-inflatable, foam-block model (which is slightly faster to deploy but bulkier to stow).

- **Towline:** Useful to essential if someone gets tired or injured (see Rescue chapter 8).

- **Signaling Devices:** Like a horn on your car, the Coast Guard requires all boaters to have a noisemaker at hand to avoid collisions with other boats, commonly a whistle on your PFD. At night a waterproof light is required. For emergencies, prepared paddlers carry small aerial flares, signal mirrors, and other devices to summon assistance from a distance.

- **Cell Phones, Marine Radios, and PLBs:** Cell phones and VHF marine radios can be useful, depending on coverage. Small waterproof radios commonly carried in a PFD pocket give direct access to the Coast Guard or other boaters nearby on Channel 16 and receive local marine weather forecasts, but they have a limited range. Personal locator beacons (PLBs) that send emergency distress signals via satellite have a much greater range.

- **Hypothermia and Bivouac Kits:** If someone becomes hypothermic, or you become stranded and need to bivouac overnight, having a way to get warm and dry could save a life. It can be as simple as wrapping up in a tarp or could include a sleeping bag, tent, backpack stove, and can of soup.

- **Float Plan:** Leave a float plan with a reliable person before you go boating. It should include where you're planning to paddle and when rescue agencies should start looking for you, along with information to help them identify you, like the color and type of kayak you have. It can be as casual as a note left on your windshield or as formal as the full Coast Guard float plan forms available online.

Section II: On-Water Skills

Fiordo Comau, Patagonia, Chile KIM GRANDFIELD

CHAPTER THREE

Launching and Landing

Before hopping into your kayak to paddle off into the sunset, take a minute to adjust your seat and foot braces.

Surf launch, Lost Coast, California SANDY RINTOUL

Fitting Your Kayak

"You don't sit in your kayak," the saying goes, "you *wear* it." Instead of slouching back like naptime in a recliner, sit upright, comfortably snug in the cockpit, so your lower body can help control the boat and transfer paddling energy more effectively. The balls of your feet push against the foot braces with knees raised and flared out to the sides, contacting the thigh braces (if your boat has them), and heels angled in toward each other and legs in a diamond shape (see photo). Ankles should be flexed so you're not on tiptoes, but not jammed uncomfortably so that your feet fall asleep. If the seat back adjusts, snug it up for back support.

Position of feet on foot braces PETER DONOHUE

Safety Note: Don't step into the cockpit. If you lose your balance while standing in the cockpit, you'll likely go down—hard.

- Instead, straddle the kayak and sit on the back deck behind the cockpit.

- With hands braced on the back deck, put your feet in the cockpit, then lift your butt up over the seat back and slide into the seat.

Getting Serious with Custom Outfitting

If your thigh braces adjust, experiment with which position gives the most edging control. Unfortunately, most adjustable thigh braces require tools, so this can't be done on the fly. Depending on sea conditions, I'll sometimes crank my foot braces a notch closer when playing in rough water. If your butt is sliding side to side when you edge, brace, or roll, consider adding hip pads.

Attaching Your Spray Skirt

Leave the skirt off until you've practiced capsizing. While releasing a skirt after a capsize isn't difficult, it's more comfortable if the first time is by design rather than by surprise (see "Wet Exit," chapter 8).

- Start in back (leaning back helps), hooking the bungee and inching forward along the sides of the cockpit rim while maintaining tension. (See paddler on left in photo below.)

- Use your forearms to pin the skirt against the coaming (cockpit rim) as you go. (See paddler on right in photo below.)

- When you get to the front, leave the grab loop sticking out. This is the "rip cord" that you pull to release the skirt when you capsize.

- If the skirt pops off in back, start over from scratch in the back.

Attaching spray skirt SANDY RINTOUL

Launching: Getting Started

Knuckle Walking

Although simple and stable, knuckle walking is somewhat limited in scope. Those with longer arms and more upper-body strength tend to find it easier.

1. Pick a gently sloping sand or gravel beach with calm water.

2. Put your bow at the edge of the water and get in.

3. Shove off your knuckles, trying to lunge and scoot yourself forward. It might help to grunt. (You can also use your paddle in one hand, like a ski pole.)

Knuckle walking with paddle PETER DONOHUE

Tip: Try putting the bow further into the water. But the more you float your boat, *the less stable it'll be*—which brings us to the next technique.

Paddle-Brace Launch

The paddle-brace method can broaden launch sites options. It works on shallow, sandy beaches as well as steeper banks, rocky shores, and off boat docks, but practice on easy beaches to work out the balance before branching out. Use your paddle as a kickstand while you clamber into the cockpit.

Straddle kayak and lean gently on paddle for balance to slide into the seat. Peter Donohue

1. On a beach with no waves or boat wakes, put the boat parallel to the shore about shin deep and straddle the cockpit.

Paddle-brace hand position with fingers of left hand in cockpit, thumb over paddle shaft
Peter Donohue

2. Hold your paddle behind you and slide the shoreward blade away from you until the other blade is almost to your left hand. Squat onto the back deck as you grab the back of the cockpit and your paddle in the left hand. It's easier if your hand is facing back so that your fingers are in the cockpit and your thumb is on the paddle shaft (see photos).

3. Slide your right hand out about a foot and lean on it *gently* for support. Be careful not to lean too much weight on your shoreward hand or there's a slight chance you could break your paddle. Your shoreward blade should rest securely on a stable surface, and both feet should still be on the ground.

4. Perched gingerly on the back deck, slide first your left leg into the cockpit, then the other leg, as you slide into the seat.

Now that you're in the boat, practice reversing the process to get back out and you've just completed the paddle-brace landing.

Getting Serious

With a little creativity, this method can be adapted to launch and land in a variety of contexts. Instead of balancing your paddle on the sand, you can use a low dock, rock, or steep bank.

Paddle-brace technique being used to balance on a rock PETER DONOHUE

On beaches with small waves or boat wakes where waves will fill your cockpit when parallel to shore, face your kayak into the waves.

Scrambles and Seal Launches

Here are a couple options to expand your repertoire.

Scramble Launch

The scramble (or cowboy/cowgirl) launch involves floating your boat, strad-dling the cockpit, and sitting down into the seat. This is faster than the previous method and great for practicing the balance and bracing skills for the scramble rescue described later.

Try it on firm ground first to see if your cockpit's big enough to get your legs in without having to worry about tipping over. If you have trouble, see "Tips for Long Legs and Little Cockpits" below.

1. Float your kayak out about knee deep. Get as deep as you can while still being able to straddle the cockpit comfortably, right over the seat. Hold your paddle in a high brace position, so you are ready to brace when you sit down.

2. Start to squat, then sit down, getting your butt down into the seat in one smooth motion to immediately lower your center of gravity, while slapping a high brace for balance.

3. Use your paddle for balance as you slide first one leg, then the other, into the cockpit; you can brace your paddle on the ground or use a *sculling high brace* if you know how.

Tip: Paddle away from shore before putting your skirt on so you don't get washed back ashore while you do it.

Scramble launch 1: Straddle cockpit and prepare to brace. Sandy Rintoul

Scramble launch 2: Sit and brace. SANDY RINTOUL

Scramble-Launch Tips for Long Legs and Little Cockpits

- Push your butt all the way back against the seat back, lean back onto the back deck, and lift your butt off the seat to gain extra legroom. Balance is an issue at this point, so using your paddle to brace is essential.

Scramble for long legs, sculling behind neck for balance SANDY RINTOUL

- You can also try hooking the heel of one foot on the front of the cockpit to push yourself back a bit farther while you slip the toe of your other foot into the cockpit. Standing on tiptoes on the foot brace with that foot helps to get your other leg in.

- Another trick is to grab your ankle with one hand to guide your foot into the cockpit; brace by putting your paddle shaft behind your neck and bracing one-handed

Seal Launch

Like knuckle walking, but with a gravity assist, slide yourself down a slope into the water—*whee!* Seal launches can be simple—*sliding a few feet down a muddy bank into a slough*—or spectacular. The size of the splash you make is up to you. It's fun, but not without inherent risks. Plant your kayak close to the tipping point of bank, rock, dock, or cliff. Attach your skirt. Brace your knees, and lunge forward into the void. Consider wearing a helmet.

Landing Techniques

Basic Landing

Landing may seem pretty basic, but I've seen more capsizes watching people try to land than just about any other maneuver. The back of your kayak is often still afloat when the front runs aground, creating an unstable situation. Paddle hard the last few strokes, trying to run your kayak high enough up the beach to create a stable platform. You can try to knuckle walk a bit farther from there, but going uphill is challenging. Using your paddle to brace in much the same way as you did for the paddle-brace launch is a good alternative.

(Un)Scramble Landing

The scramble (or unscramble) landing is my favorite for most situations because it's quick, and on rocky beaches you can stand up in the shallows before your boat scrapes onto the rocks. As you approach shore, get your feet out of the cockpit. The same tricks described above for getting your feet into the kayak work for getting them out. The key is to leave your butt in your seat until you get your feet out, as opposed to trying to sit on the back deck first. Put your paddle across your lap and stand up when it's shallow enough to do so, grabbing your paddle out of your lap before it falls.

Scramble landing 1: Pull feet out of cockpit as you approach the shore. SANDY RINTOUL

Scramble landing 2 SANDY RINTOUL

Surf Launches and Landings

Launching or landing on beaches with surf bigger than 1 foot is recommended only for L3 and above paddlers with previous instruction who are wearing helmets. Keep your kayak facing directly perpendicular to the waves as you paddle out. The upper limit of L4 is 3-foot surf, which will be just over head high to a seated kayaker, and landing in surf this high generally requires the ability to brace and *side surf*. If you're not sure what this means, it means you should pick a different beach. If you happen to get caught out and need to land through surf, you might jump out of your boat at the surf line and swim and wade your kayak in. Be careful not to get between your kayak and shore in surf, which can slam your boat into your body with astounding force.

Punching through L4 surf on the Lost Coast, California. SANDY RINTOUL

CHAPTER FOUR

Basic Strokes and Maneuvers: Getting Started

A big attraction to paddling kayaks is their maneuverability. Sometimes, however, this extreme maneuverability can feel like a liability, and making your kayak go where *you* want it to go—rather than where *it* seems to want to go—seems like a game of tug-o-war. Understanding a few key concepts can put you back in the driver's seat instead of feeling like you're being taken for a ride.

Costa Verde, Brazil. CHRISTIAN FUCHS

How to Hold Your Paddle: Getting Started with Tips on Grip

Your boat will go even if you're holding your paddle upside-down and backwards; but like a spoon, most paddles have a specific orientation that's most effective. Unless your blades are symmetrical, as with Greenland paddles, they have a *face* and a *back*. (**Note:** Although these tips will work for getting started with a GP, see "Tips for Sticks" in chapter 7 for nuances in technique.)

- Hold the paddle with the scooped *face* toward you and the longer lobe on top (designed so that when immersed at a paddling angle, the pressure evens out on the blade face).

- For good leverage, use a fairly wide grip, with hands outside of shoulder width at a minimum.

- A slightly wider, more performance-oriented grip can be achieved with the paddle on your head and sliding your hands out until your elbows are at right angles (see photo). This affords more leverage and power and encourages more of the all-important "torso rotation."

- For a vertical blade angle, line your knuckles up with the top of the blade (with only your control hand if using a *feathered* paddle).

- To prevent muscle strain, keep hands loose and relaxed, with wrists straight rather than cocked.

A wide grip encourages torso rotation. Peter Donohue

Knuckles lined up with top of blade PETER DONOHUE

For Feathered Friends: With feathered paddles, realign your grip for each stroke on the non-control (usually left) side. Instead of cocking your control-hand (right) wrist backwards, maintain a straight wrist while lifting your right fist toward your ear (as if to punch yourself), allowing the shaft to spin in your left hand until your knuckles line up with the top of the blade. Take a stroke, and let the shaft spin back in the left hand. "Righty-tighty, lefty loose-y" is used to describe this move.

The Forward Stroke: Getting Started

Instead of bicycling away with your forearms, get the feel of torso rotation by trying this:

- Sitting in your kayak with paddle held out about arm's length and shoulder height, swing it side to side several times.

- As you do this, reach forward, put the paddle in the water, and pull on it as you rotate your torso back—taking a forward stroke. Keep rotating and planting your paddle on each side to paddle forward, leaving arms fairly straight to maintain your power box (see page 48).

- Focus more on pushing with the top hand than pulling with the bottom, to engage stronger muscle groups.

- To go straighter, keep the stroke short and in front of you, toes to hips. The farther behind your hips you go, the more your kayak will tend to turn.

Forward stroke 1: Wind up and plant near toes. PETER DONOHUE

Forward stroke 2: Unwind to hips. PETER DONOHUE

The Brakes: Getting Started to Stop

When stopping or backing, use the back of the blade, not the face. For a simple stop, reach back, jam the back of the blade into the water at the hip, and hold it there; the kayak will turn to that side.

Tip: For a quicker stop in a straight line, change sides when the boat starts to turn. Do this back and forth a few times until you stop.

Putting on the brakes PETER DONOHUE

Reverse Stroke: Getting Started Going Backwards

A basic reverse stroke uses a similar motion to stopping, but you reach farther back. (See video at EskapeKayak.com/instructional-videos/skills-drills-instructional-videos/.)

- Rotate your torso to the right, reaching back and planting the back of the blade flat on the water to give some balance support.

Reverse stroke: Rotate back to plant blade flat. PETER DONOHUE

- Push down and out to the side with the back of the blade, unwinding your torso.

- The right blade comes out around your knees, and you continue to rotate back to take a stroke on the left.

- Looking back to plant the blade encourages torso rotation and lets you see behind you.

- To go straighter paddle gently at first until you gain momentum.

Forward Sweep Stroke: Getting Started Turning

Putting the brakes on one side, as when stopping, will turn your kayak, but your halting, stop-start progress will be tiring and inefficient. The *forward sweep* is a more effective alternative because it both turns your kayak and propels it forward.

- Rotate forward to plant the right blade at your feet, as if for a forward stroke. As you rotate back, reach out to the side as far as possible, then back toward the stern, in a wide, rainbow arc.

Forward sweep: Reach out wide to turn. Sandy Rintoul

- Don't rush it. Give your kayak time to turn. A quality sweep stroke can take twice as long as a forward stroke.

- Like the forward stroke, the power for the sweep comes from torso rotation and pushing with the opposite hand. Pushing your foot on the same side as the stroke gives extra oomph.

- Turning your head and watching the blade through a full, 180-degree arc to the stern can enhance your torso rotation. But in actual use, you'll usually look where you're going and end the stroke before the stern, unless you're doing a *spin turn*.

Reverse Sweep Stroke and Spin Turns

The *reverse sweep stroke* is the opposite of a forward sweep, using the same elements: wide, 180-degree arc, only this time from stern to bow. They stop forward momentum, so use them in situations where turning is more important than maintaining speed, such as to avoid running into something. They're also used to steer when paddling in reverse, but they're really useful for spinning in place.

Spin Turn

For quick turn-arounds in tight quarters, combine reverse sweeps alternately with forward sweeps. (See video at EskapeKayak.com/instructional-videos/skills-drills-instructional-videos/.)

1. Starting with a reverse sweep, rotate back to the right, and plant the back of your paddle flat (for balance) by the rear hatch.

2. Turn the flat blade vertical as you push out away from the stern in a wide arc all the way to your toes, initiating a spin to the right.

3. Reach forward on the left and do a forward sweep.

4. Keep alternating right-hand reverse sweeps with left-hand forward sweeps to spin in place 180 degrees.

   Tip: Use wide, slow strokes. If you're splashing, it means turning energy is going to waste.

   Tip: Edging during sweeps makes them more efficient (see next chapter).

Sweep Stroke + Forward Stroke Combination: Getting More Efficient

Interspersing forward sweep strokes every few forward strokes helps keep your kayak going straight, sweeping when it starts to veer off course. Instead of taking several sweeps on one side, maintaining your right-left paddling rhythm, as described below, will be more efficient.

- To turn left, combine a wide, long sweep on the right, followed by a short, vertical forward stroke on the left.

- Do this sweep-stroke and forward-stroke combination as you gradually steer back on course.

- Keep your forward strokes close to the boat and short, ending at the hip, to minimize their turning effect.

- Make constant small corrections to *stay* on course rather than big corrections to *get back* on course. As soon as you start to veer, do a sweep stroke on that side, trying not to get more than one sweep stroke off course. (You could also drop your rudder or skeg if you have one, but if they malfunction, it's good to know how to control your kayak without one.)

- To steer most effectively, put your kayak on edge as you sweep (see next chapter).

Stern Rudder: Another Way to Turn

If you're still off course after two or three sweep-stroke/forward-stroke combinations, try a *stern rudder*. Reach back and do the first few inches of a back sweep and you'll have the essence of the stern rudder.

Tip: Instead of pushing out to the side and creating a big braking action, rotate your torso back so the blade stays nearly parallel to the stern and push gently against the back of the blade, taking advantage of your momentum to turn. It's still a braking stroke, but go as light on the brakes as possible.

The Nudge: Stern Rudder + Forward Sweep

To minimize the breaking effect of the stern rudder, follow it with a forward sweep.

Stern rudder to correct course PETER DONOHUE

Using stern rudder to surf a wave SANDY RINTOUL

- Plant a stern rudder on the right, just enough to "nudge" your bow until it just starts to turn.

- Follow this stern-rudder nudge quickly with a forward sweep on the left to regain some lost momentum. By first nudging the bow to the right, your sweep will have more effect, and speed loss will be minimized.

Bracing for Support: Getting Started Staying Upright

You might plan to steer clear of waves and rough water, but an unexpected gust or boat wake can quickly turn your well-planned calm-water cruise from nice thrill to nightmare unless you know how to brace. Bracing skills expand your safety margin and comfort level, as well as the range of areas you can explore safely.

The most basic braces involve slapping your paddle flat against the water for momentary support to maintain or regain your balance in bumpy seas.

- Without changing your grip, with knuckles lined up with the top of the blade, reach out to the side with the face of the blade and gently push straight down against the surface. Feel the resistance as you push down a foot or so. You'll also feel resistance lifting a flat blade back up through the water; shed this resistance by turning the blade vertical to slice it back up to the surface.

- Now try it with the back of the blade, pushing down to feel resistance and slicing the blade vertically back to the surface.

- Next try slapping the water a little harder with the face and then the back of the blade; feel the support.

Although a quick slap is better than nothing, bracing is more effective when combined with the edging and bracing techniques described in the next chapter.

Basic bracing: slapping the surface with a flat blade PETER DONOHUE

CHAPTER FIVE

Advanced Strokes and Maneuvers: Getting Serious

A smooth sea never made a skillful mariner.
—*Anonymous*

Refining your strokes so they're more efficient and effective is the focus of this chapter, with an emphasis on edging and bracing that will help you push your edges more comfortably in rougher water.

Low brace to land in surf EDUARDO SALDIAS

General Paddling Concepts

Key concepts common to all strokes;

- **Torso rotation** refers to using the large muscles of your back, torso, and legs, in addition to your arms.
- **Power box** is the box shape between your chest, arms, and paddle when holding the paddle away from your body with elbows bent less than 90 degrees. Imagine paddling with a small child on your lap, and don't crush the baby with your paddle shaft. This position enhances leverage and torso rotation.
- **Bury the blade.** Submerge the entire blade before applying power to get the most out of your paddle. "Anchor the blade" and try to pull the boat to your paddle rather than pulling the paddle through the water. It's a subtle but important difference.
- **Four basic phases** of each stroke:
  1. **Wind-up:** Torso is rotated like coiling a spring.
  2. **Catch:** Blade is buried and anchored.
  3. **Power Phase:** Torso unwinds as boat gets pulled to the paddle.
  4. **Recovery:** Stroke is finished and paddle pulled from the water.

High-Angle Forward Stroke: Getting Serious *Fast*

Developing an efficient forward stroke is a lifelong project. Kayak racers spend entire careers chasing the "perfect" stroke, but even the most relaxed recreational paddlers can gain more distance with less effort by paying attention to basic biomechanics and kinesiology. (Traditional paddlers, see "Tips for Sticks," chapter 7.) Whether you're out to win races or just beat the afternoon wind back to shore, a foundation in the high-angle racing stroke is great to have when you need to get somewhere fast. For casual touring, the intensity of this powerful sprinting stroke can be dialed down while still preserving the efficiency.

Start by sitting up straight, or with your upper body canted slightly forward for more powerful torso rotation. (See video at EskapeKayak.com/instructional-videos/skills-drills-instructional-videos/.)

High-angle forward stroke: Wind-up and catch PETER DONOHUE

1. **Wind-up:** With your hands held out about shoulder height, rotate your left shoulder forward, along with your entire torso. Imagine a searchlight shining from your navel—aimed to at least two o'clock so that your torso is wound up like a pitcher about to throw a fastball. Pushing off your right foot brace will enhance this.

2. **Catch:** With torso still coiled, spear your left blade into the water next to your feet as far forward as you can without leaning forward, and as soon as your blade is fully submerged . . .

3. **Power Phase:** Unwind your torso by simultaneously pushing off your left foot brace, pulling back on the left blade, and pushing forward and across your body with the right hand. This hand stays high, crossing in front of your face from chin to forehead height, as if wiping a foggy windshield (rather than plunging downward), for the most effective blade angle. Preserve your power box (don't crush the baby!) by not bending your elbows more than 90 degrees.

4. **Recovery:** When your left hand reaches your hip and your torso has uncoiled to neutral, slice the blade straight up out of the water (rather than bending your elbow and pulling back so you scoop water), and begin to wind up to the right, still pushing off your left foot brace.

High-angle forward stroke: power phase Peter Donohue

High-angle forward stroke: recovery Peter Donohue

5. **Wind-up on right:** Rotate your right shoulder forward, shine your belly button light at ten o'clock, and prepare to plant your right blade and push off your right foot brace.

Tips and Common Mistakes

- Push off the foot brace on the same side as the stroke.

- Relax the grip on your top hand. Opening your hand slightly as you push gives your forearms a brief break, reducing muscle strain.

- "If you swoop, you scoop." Keep the top hand about eye level without "swooping" (pushing down toward your deck), which changes your blade angle so it ends up "scooping" (lifting water rather than pushing you forward).

- Bury the blade on the catch *before* pulling on it. A common mistake is to start unwinding while planting the blade so it doesn't get fully immersed until the stroke is half over.

- Don't rock forward and back with your upper body or side to side. A "quiet" boat is a faster boat.

- Instead of digging deeper, harder, and longer, use a shorter stroke with a higher cadence. An average touring cadence for 3 knots is around 60 strokes per minute. To sprint, think "spinning" on a bicycle, increasing your cadence to around 80 strokes per minute or more; the average cadence for an Olympic sprint racer is over 120 strokes per minute!

Touring Stroke Tip

For longer distances, you can relax the high-angle stroke, but the same efficiency concepts apply. Hold your hands lower, from shoulder to mid-chest height, but you still use the torso.

Edging

Learning to put your kayak comfortably on edge is a core skill for getting beyond the basics. From basic turning to the most advanced maneuvers—all are enhanced by edging. Getting your kayak up on edge makes it want to dance!

Edging vs. Leaning: Getting Started

To understand what edging is, it's helpful to understand what it's not. Sitting up straight in your kayak, or in your chair as you read this, your nose should be lined up with your belly button. This *nose-over-navel* alignment is an important concept. In contrast, tilt your head to the right and start to move it to the side until your nose is lined up over your right knee. If you keep moving your head and *leaning* in this direction, you'll eventually fall out of your chair.

To *edge* rather than *lean*, shift your weight onto your right bun cheek while angling your head toward your left shoulder, keeping the nose-over-navel alignment. As you shift farther right, start lifting your left knee, bending your body into a C shape. You'll feel a tightening on your left side—edging essentially involves doing side crunches.

On-Water Edging Exercises

Level 1 edging: Weight shifted slightly to one cheek PETER DONOHUE

Three-Levels-of-Edging Balance Drill

In this classic drill you'll practice holding your kayak on edge so you can do things like carve through a turn. Basically, you hold your kayak for several seconds at each level. Until your bracing skills are solid, practice by using a paddle float or by resting your paddle on a partner's bow so you don't tip over.

- Start by holding your kayak at level 1 for 5 seconds.

- Then hold level 2 for 5 seconds, then level 3, back to level 2, and back to level 1. Switch sides.

Level 2 edging: Near 45 degrees, most sea kayaks on edge have some degree of inherent "secondary stability," built into the design, a sweet spot where it likes to balance and where the magic starts to happen. Note the "nose-over-navel" alignment of the head. PETER DONOHUE

Level 3 edging: The teetering point on the razor's edge of capsize. PETER DONOHUE

It's common for your boat to wobble, but the goal is to hold each edge as steady as possible. As you get more comfortable, practice holding each edge for 10 seconds or more at each level. If using a paddle float or partner's bow, try not to lean on it; it's there just in case. The next step is learning to high-brace (see below) so you can ditch the training wheels and practice this drill while paddling forward.

C-to-C: Pre-Bracing Drill

This exercise isolates the C-to-C, or hip snap, body motions used for bracing.

Tip: Using a paddle float or partner's bow, edge (on right) just beyond level 3 so that you'd fall over if you weren't leaning on something. If you can't keep your nose over your navel, just do your best. Your left side will be crunched into a C shape—left knee raised, head tilted with left ear toward left shoulder, and left elbow to left hip.

Next, recover your balance by quickly doing a crunch on your right side— contracting at the waist to bring your right knee up while dropping your right ear toward your right shoulder as you push down on your paddle and drop your right elbow to your right hip. This C-to-C movement (C on left to C on right) rocks your kayak back into balance beneath you. Lean out farther and farther as you feel comfortable (see "Extreme Edging," page 108).

C-to-C 1: Edge and . . . Peter Donohue

C-to-C 2: ... hip snap, to rock the kayak back under you. Peter Donohue

Bracing: Getting Serious

Adding this hip-snap motion to the support gained from slapping the water with a flat blade (introduced in the previous chapter) creates a more effective brace. This style of brace has four parts: edge, slap, snap, and recover (analogous to the wind-up, catch, power phase, and recovery of other strokes). However much a brace may look like you're using your paddle to push your body back up over your boat, it's important to understand that braces are more effective if you're actually planting your paddle against the surface, *then using your knees and hips to rock your kayak back underneath you*, using a C-to-C motion.

High Brace

The high brace uses the face of the blade, like the forward stroke. Its name refers to your hands being held *higher* than your elbows.

Find the high-brace position by dropping your elbows to your sides and holding the paddle shaft below shoulder height near your chest as if you'd just done a pull-up. By dropping your elbows down to bring your hands up, your blade face will be horizontal, ready to smack the water without your having to change your grip (by spinning the shaft in your hands). **Note:** With a feathered paddle, you will have to first spin the shaft into position on the left as if taking a forward stroke on that side. (See video at EskapeKayak.com/instructional-videos/skills-drills-instructional-videos/.)

1. **Edge:** With elbows down and paddle horizontal, edge right into the C position.

2. **Slap:** As you teeter off balance, smack the face of the right blade against the surface, using the brief support to . . .

3. **Snap:** Do a hip snap, rocking the kayak back under you by crunching into a C on the right.

4. **Recovery:** After the quick slap-snap phase, recover your paddle by slicing it back up to the surface. The paddle should end up back in paddling position, with the blade face toward the back.

Caution! How to High Brace Safely

Because of the potential for shoulder injury with improperly performed high braces, some instructors don't teach them, and this is certainly the safest strategy. Most of these instructors do teach rolling, however, essentially a form of high brace. It's an extremely powerful tool when used correctly, but like any power tool, it can be dangerous when wielded improperly.

To avoid injury, keep high braces low and in front of you: hands below shoulders and elbows tucked to your sides as if clutching $100 bills in your armpits. **Especially important:** Keep hands in front of the plane of your shoulders. Allowing the hand on your bracing side to float up and behind your head in a throwing motion places the shoulder joint at risk.

High brace 1: edge . . . PETER DONOHUE

High brace 2: slap . . . PETER DONOHUE

High brace 3: hip snap and . . . PETER DONOHUE

High brace 4: recovery PETER DONOHUE

High brace in surf EDUARDO SALDIAS

Low Brace

The low brace uses the back of the blade, like the reverse stroke, with hands held *lower* than elbows. As with the high brace, don't change your grip or bend your wrists. From paddling position, drop the paddle shaft toward your belly button, leaving elbows up, directly over fists. The back of the blade will be flat to the water, and wrists will be straight.

1. **Edge:** Get into the low-brace "monkey" position, with elbows up, and edge right into a C.

2. **Slap:** Smack the back of the right blade against the surface, using the momentary support to snap.

3. **Snap:** Do a hip snap, rocking the kayak back under you by crunching into a C on the right.

4. **Recovery:** After the quick slap-snap phase, recover your paddle by slicing it back up to normal paddling position.

Low brace 1–2: edge and slap . . . PETER DONOHUE

Low brace 2–3: slap and snap! PETER DONOHUE

Low brace 4: recovery PETER DONOHUE

High or Low? Which to Use When

Low braces are hands down the more powerful and safer choice, using a stronger, more stable body position, albeit one that's limited in scope. Since they use the back of the blade, they work well toward the end of your stroke or if you want to look behind you in choppy seas. In this case they can be applied preventively—by planting the brace *before* looking back. Think of them as your first line of defense. This hands-down position, however, only allows you to edge so far. Once you tip much beyond 45 degrees, the blade starts sinking and low braces become increasingly ineffective.

High braces are particularly useful toward the beginning of your stroke if you need support as you reach out to plant the face of the blade. But their full potential is realized when your skills and balance improve and you find yourself well up on edge, with your kayak approaching 90 degrees or more. With practice you can learn to catch yourself on a high brace after your low brace has completely failed, giving you a second line of defense.

Sculling High Brace

Instead of the fleeting support offered by slapping the water, sculling involves skimming the blade back and forth repeatedly across the surface to create a sustained brace. This is useful for getting your legs into the cockpit during scramble launches and rescues.

Sculling brace 1: Sculling back toward stern with blade at a slight climbing angle
PETER DONOHUE

Sculling brace 2: Sculling forward with climbing angle toward bow PETER DONOHUE

1. Rest the face of the blade on the water about even with your knees. Angle the blade so that as you start to move it toward the stern, it skims the surface; this is called putting a "climbing angle" on the "leading edge." Rotate your torso back, skimming the paddle behind you (rotating your torso instead of reaching back keeps your shoulder in a safe position).

2. Now switch the leading edge (so the part toward the bow is lifted, but still using the face of the blade) and rotate forward, skimming forward to its starting position at your knees. Continue skimming back and forth, using the face of the paddle as you gradually edge onto your paddle and feel the support. It's common to start sculling frantically back and forth as if dancing the twist. But instead of Chubby Checkers, slow down and think "Waltzing Matilda": sculling back (one-two-three) and forward (one-two-three) in wide, smooth arcs.

Deep Sculling on Back

Referred to as *side sculling* or *Greenland sculling*, this maneuver is an excellent way to develop the blade finesse and body positions used in rolling. It's easiest to learn this challenging maneuver with a partner. (See video at Eskape Kayak.com/instructional-videos/skills-drills-instructional-videos/.)

Sculling on back with partner stabilizing PETER DONOHUE

1. Grabbing your deck lines, your partner keeps your kayak from tipping beyond 45 degrees as you lie back onto the water and begin sculling.

2. Keep the blade skimming nearly flat, sculling slowly from perpendicular almost to the bow rather than letting it drift behind you.

3. As you find your balance, your partner begins letting go. Arch your back to keep the kayak from rocking past 45 degrees and rolling onto you.

Tips

- An extended paddle position (holding the paddle at the end of the blade, see page 82) gives you more leverage and is easier.

- Commit your head and back completely to floating on the water. Get your shoulder blades flat on the water and lay your head back to "put your chin in the air and your eyebrows in the water," as rolling guru Helen Wilson explains it.

- It helps to be flexible and to use a kayak with a low back deck.

Sweep Strokes with Edging: Carving Turns

Sea kayaks are designed to track straight when flat and to turn when edged. Take advantage of this by carving turns instead of fighting a flat boat using sweep strokes alone. To turn right, sweep on the left while lifting your right knee to put your kayak on its left edge. It can be confusing to remember which knee to lift, so just reach out on your sweep stroke to increase leverage.

Tips

- By reaching far out with his right blade, the paddler below automatically lifts his left knee and puts the kayak on the right (correct) edge for him to turn to his left. Angling the blade to blend some high brace with a sweep stroke will be covered in the next chapter.

- The paddler maintains a comfortable (level 2) edge, taking advantage of the kayak's secondary stability, as he finishes the sweep and takes another left forward stroke.

- Continue alternating right sweeps with left forward strokes while maintaining your edge, continuing to carve a turn without rocking back to flat with each forward stroke.

Reaching out wide to sweep puts the kayak on the correct edge, in this case for turning to his left. PETER DONOHUE

Draw Strokes: Getting Started Going Sideways

Using *draw strokes* to move sideways is handy for *rafting up* (maneuvering two or more kayaks parallel together), to chat, check the chart, or stabilize for a rescue. One thing the many types of draw strokes have in common: A vertical paddle is more efficient. (See video at EskapeKayak.com/instructional-videos/skills-drills-instructional-videos/.)

Standard Draw

The basic version of draw stroke (aka draw to the hip or beam draw).

1. Reach your paddle to the side at arm's length and turn the blade face parallel to the kayak's side. Turn your torso to "face your work," getting your paddle shaft as vertical as possible by reaching your top hand out over the water about forehead height.

2. Plant the blade and pull it toward your hip (actually, you'll pull the kayak toward the paddle), using only your bottom hand and leaving your top hand in place as a pivot point.

3. As the blade gets close to your kayak, either:
    a. lift it out of the water by letting it slice straight up behind you and then reach out for another stroke (this "out-of-water recovery" is easier); or

Draw stroke 1: Reach out. Sandy Rintoul

Draw stroke 2: Pull in. Sandy Rintoul

Draw stroke 3: Turn and slice back out. Sandy Rintoul

b. instead of lifting the blade out of the water, rotate it quickly 90 degrees (blade face toward the back) and slice it back out to arm's length to take another stroke, leaving the blade submerged the whole time. (This "in-water recovery" is more efficient.)

Tip: With either version, lift (or rotate) the blade *before it catches against the side of your kayak*, or you could trip over it. To avoid capsizing if this does happen, let go with your top hand and allow the blade to fall away from you.

Sculling Draw: Getting More Serious

The sculling motion used to provide continuous support during the sculling brace can also be used with a vertical paddle shaft to create a continuous sideways motion. Like the sculling brace, getting the blade angle just right can be challenging at first; but once you get the feel for it, the sculling draw is the most effective way to move sideways. (See video at EskapeKayak.com/instructional-videos/skills-drills-instructional-videos/.)

1. Start with the easier sculling brace—skimming the water out to the side with the blade face. Continue sculling as you slowly move your paddle into a vertical, draw-stroke position with both hands out over the water.

2. Again, turn to "face your work," keeping your bottom hand low, almost touching the water.

3. Center the stroke on your hip, sculling from your knee to a foot or so behind you.

Tip: Don't over-rotate your blade angle. Keep it skimming nearly parallel to the boat. The goal is to make the boat go straight sideways instead of spinning at an angle. Mastering sculling is the key to advanced maneuvers like bow rudder, side slip, and rolling.

CHAPTER SIX

Maneuvers and Blended Strokes

Sea kayaking is about how and when the strokes described previously are put together to get you where you want to go. Most skilled kayakers are constantly blending strokes along the way, adding a bit of sweep stroke to the end of a forward stroke to stay on course and maybe adding a braced sweep to feel more stable edging. Here are a few common maneuvers and blends.

Using a braced sideslip to keep from washing into the wall Kim Grandfield

Flattening the blade to create a braced sweep stroke PETER DONOHUE

Getting Serious: Braced Sweep Strokes

For added stability on edge, especially in choppy seas, blend in a little bracing by angling your blade toward a high-brace position during forward sweeps. Start with your paddle angled at 45 degrees and experiment. Less angle (a more vertical blade) gives less support but more turning power; more angle gives more support but less turning power—although more edge will increase your turning ability. Developing a feel for how much bracing angle to use, and when, takes practice and is part of the art of paddling.

Turning Spin Turns into Low-Brace Turns

To spin more quickly, edge toward each sweep stroke, using braced sweep strokes for stability: high brace with forward sweep, low brace with reverse sweep. With forward momentum, use a braced reverse sweep to do a low-brace turn, one of the more elegant maneuvers in kayaking.

1. To turn right, get some momentum, edge, and sweep left using a braced sweep to "initiate the turn" (an important concept used for most maneuvers) to start carving right on the left edge.

2. Rotate your torso to face right, positioning the paddle for a low brace on that side slightly behind you (about four o'clock).

3. Edge toward the right blade until it contacts the water, allowing it to skim across the surface with a slight climbing angle, creating both support and some drag that begins a gentle, gliding right turn.

Low-Brace Turnaround

To turn around in a big hurry—to get back to a capsized partner or face an approaching wave before it breaks—combine the low-brace turn with a reverse sweep stroke, then blend it into a spin turn. (See video at Eskape Kayak.com/instructional-videos/skills-drills-instructional-videos/.)

1. Initiate a right turn as above, edging on a braced sweep on the left.

2. This time plant the low brace back at the 5:30 position. Rotate until both hands are low over the water, front hand nearly getting wet.

3. As you edge onto the low brace, don't push down too hard; instead, skim the blade across the surface, creating an outrigger as you "ride the glide" for a couple seconds, allowing your boat to turn using forward momentum (see photo 1 below).

4. As you feel yourself starting to sink at the end of the glide, push gradually down and out to the side smoothly to both regain your balance and continue the turn—using a braced, reverse sweep stroke *all the way to the bow* (see photo 2, next page).

5. Continue into a spin turn, reaching forward on the left, alternating forward and reverse braced sweeps to turn around.

Low-brace turnaround 1: riding the glide PETER DONOHUE

Low-brace turnaround 2: pushing the back of the blade forward into a reverse sweep
PETER DONOHUE

Tip: See how far on edge you can get (the goal is getting the spray skirt in the water), going farther and farther until you capsize. To discover your limits, you have to exceed them.

Bow Rudders: Maneuvering

Developed by whitewater slalom racers who need to make efficient and precise course corrections, bow rudders come in handy for sea kayakers as well. Use them to reach a partner's bow more efficiently during T rescues and for maneuvering in tight quarters like mangrove channels and sea caves. Creating less braking action than stern rudders, which turn you by pushing the stern sideways (like the back wheels of a rear-wheel-drive car skidding sideways on ice), bow rudders actually draw your bow toward the turn (like front-wheel drive).

Assuming the Position

The bow rudder is essentially a draw stroke that relies on forward momentum, using the same blade angle as a sculling draw.

- To find the blade angle and body position for a bow rudder, start with a vertical, sculling draw slowly on your right. When sculling toward the bow, the blade faces you with its leading edge (bottom of the blade) angled away from the bow slightly, *no more* than one o'clock.

Bow rudder to approach a capsized kayak . . . SANDY RINTOUL

. . . using momentum to turn and glide over to the bow SANDY RINTOUL

- Maintain this one o'clock angle while leaning forward slightly and moving the blade forward to about your knee, a foot from the kayak. Lift your right knee to edge away from the stroke. That's the basic position of your blade and body. All you need now is momentum.

- To get a feel of what this subtle maneuver feels like, hold the position while someone standing at your stern pushes you gently forward into a turn.

Adding Momentum and Initiating a Turn

The full stroke-blend combination for this maneuver is sweep left, bow rudder right, forward stroke right. (See video at EskapeKayak.com/instructional-videos/skills-drills-instructional-videos/.)

1. Get momentum, edge, and sweep left to initiate a carved right turn.

2. Keep edging and carving as you plant the right blade by your knee in the "open-faced" one o'clock angle. You'll feel a slight tug on the blade as it begins to pull the bow right, tightening the turn. If you feel a lot of force on the blade, you've probably rotated it out too far (to two or three o'clock), which kills your speed.

3. After turning about 45 degrees, but before losing much momentum, transition your bow rudder quickly into a forward stroke to regain the speed lost during the turn. To do this, slice your blade forward to your feet (still at the one o'clock angle) then spin it back into a forward stroke.

Tips for Fine-Tuning and Common Mistakes

- Planting by the knee turns your boat quicker because it creates more of a pivot point for your kayak to spin around. By reaching farther forward toward your ankle, most kayaks will carve a longer, giant-slalom sort of turn and carry a bit more speed. Depending on what obstacles you're trying to avoid, having both versions in your skill set can be useful.

- Keep your kayak edged throughout the maneuver, without allowing it to flatten out as you reach across to plant the bow rudder.

- Keep your lower elbow tucked down and in (near your hip if planting the blade at your *knee*, toward the thigh when reaching farther forward).

- Remember that a bow rudder is a type of draw stroke, so like all draws, keep it vertical and use the face of the blade rather than the back.

- Keep the entire blade fully submerged, not just the tip.
- Some paddlers drop their top hand to their (right) shoulder to move the pivot point forward, but this makes the transition to the forward stroke awkward; the slalom racers who invented the maneuver don't do it.

Side Slips

A *side slip* (or *hanging draw*) is essentially the same stroke as a bow rudder—with the same open-faced, one o'clock blade angle—only you place it back at your hip instead of your knee. It's used to glide your whole kayak diagonally sideways a few feet *without actually changing your bow direction*, letting it slide *away* from an obstacle or *toward* something, such as a dock where you want to land or a capsized kayak. (See video at EskapeKayak.com/instructional-videos/skills-drills-instructional-videos/.)

1. With momentum, blend a forward stroke on the right into a side slip. Just as the right blade reaches your hip at the end of your forward stroke, quickly cock your wrist outward and into a side slip position. Getting the one o'clock blade angle is key and can be challenging at first.
2. Glide sideways several feet and resume paddling.

Side slip to glide diagonally sideways . . . Sandy Rintoul

. . . without turning the kayak. PETER DONOHUE

Side slip being used to avoid sea cave wall BUCK JOHNSON

Tips and Common Mistakes:

- Both blade placement and angle off the hip are crucial. If you turn toward the blade (like a bow rudder), the blade is too far forward. Each kayak is different, so experiment with finding the "sweet spot" where yours drifts sideways without turning.

- Don't expect too much. You might only drift a boat width before losing speed, but it may be all you need to avoid or approach your object.

Draw on the Move

Burly cousin to the graceful side slip, it's good when you need a sudden shift to the side to avoid a submerged rock. It's quicker but uses more energy than the side slip. As the name suggests, you use the *draw-to-the-hip* motion while moving forward.

Cross-Bow Rudder

One advantage to cross-bow rudders is they use more skeletal support, and therefore less energy, than a standard bow rudder. But they require more flexibility and balance, so practicing them is a great way to improve both. Cross-bow rudders are especially useful immediately *following* a bow rudder when

Cross-bow rudder SANDY RINTOUL

maneuvering in tight quarters (see below). (See video at EskapeKayak.com/instructional-videos/skills-drills-instructional-videos/.)

1. Get momentum, edge, and sweep left to initiate a right turn.

2. Reach the left blade across the bow and plant the cross-bow rudder by your right calf at the one o'clock position open-faced so that water hits the blade face.

3. Maintain edge on the left so your boat continues to carve.

4. As your glide starts to wane, you're all wound up to reach back across your deck with your left blade and blend into a left forward sweep stroke to regain momentum and continue the turn. Keep edging as you do so.

CHAPTER SEVEN

Tips for Sticks: Getting Serious with Traditional Paddles

Anyone wanting to get serious about sea kayaking, especially rolling, should definitely pick up a stick, although this is not at all to imply that you can't also paddling using a traditional paddle if just getting started. The longer, narrower blades encourage a softer paddling style that promotes finesse and the

Cate Hawthorne running a "pour over" with a stick, somewhere on the Mendocino Coast
PETER DONOHUE

development of a better "feel" for the blades. Learning traditional skills such as a variety of rolls, the sliding stroke, and extended paddle positions gives you additional tools to apply with your fat blade. Although there are various traditional-style paddles, we'll focus on the more commonly used Greenland paddles, or GPs.

While there isn't one "correct" forward-stroke technique for sticks (any more than there is with Euro "spoons"), and you might paddle blissfully ignorant for years (as I did) using basically the same technique as with a spoon, there are subtle differences. Besides being longer and narrower, sticks are thicker, giving the blades a three-dimensionality and buoyancy. Without delving too deeply into hydrodynamics and the vagaries of vortices and such, let's just say they interact somewhat differently with the water, which affects how they can be used most efficiently. The forward stroke tends to be out to the side and shorter, more akin to a low-angle touring stroke, although higher angles are used as well. One of the biggest differences is the grip.

Getting a Grip on a Stick

The grip tends to be narrower, with the paddle held lower and closer to the body.

1. Hold the stick at shoulder height across your collar bones, as if you'd just done a chin-up. Your hands should be just beyond shoulder width and elbows held loosely at your sides.

OK grip Peter Donohue

2. Now drop your hands down toward your lap until your forearms are parallel to the ground. This is perhaps a bit on the low and too-close-to-your-stomach end of the spectrum, but pretty close to the position you're aiming for.

3. If your paddle has a loom (a flattened part in the middle before the blades begin to flare), move your hands closer together to hold it on the loom. Make the OK sign with the thumb and forefinger of each hand. Now slide your OK sign out to the shoulder where the blades begin so that your thumb and forefinger are still on the loom, but when you close the last three fingers, they're resting on the beginnings of the blades. Assuming that your paddle is properly sized for you, your hands will be just beyond shoulder width.

4. For the canted forward stroke, instead of lining your knuckles up with the top edge of the blades (as with a Euro, so the blades are vertical), hold the paddle so the beginnings of the blades rest comfortably against your palms when your wrists are straight. The top of the blades will be angled forward, and they'll be lined up closer to your first finger joints than your knuckles. The angle depends on personal preference and how your paddle performs, and experimenting with the angle may decrease or increase flutter.

GP grip with top of blade angled forward Peter Donohue

Canted Forward Stroke

While it might seem counterintuitive that an angled blade would be more efficient, the long, buoyant blades create lift when canted, much like a boat propeller. In Greenland, in fact, experienced kayakers consider a paddle held with no angle to be a "beginner stroke."

1. **Wind-up:** Rotate the torso forward on the right, though less dramatically than described for Euro blades.

2. **Catch:** Slice the right blade quickly down into the water, nearly to your hand, to submerge most of the blade.

3. **Power Phase:** Unwind your torso, pushing off the right foot brace as before. When sprinting, Greenland racers often add a slight crunch forward to each stroke, something that Euro-blade racers avoid. (See videos of top racers at qajaqusa.org/Movies/movies.html.)

4. **Recovery:** Allow the buoyant blade to arc back to the surface and pop out of the water when your hand reaches your hip (although the longer blade may now be somewhat behind you).

Sliding Stroke

Instead of feathered paddles for dealing with strong winds, traditional paddlers use "storm paddles"—short sticks only as long as one's outstretched arms—along with a sliding stroke, basically shuffling the paddle side to side between each stroke. By sliding the top hand to the end of the paddle on each stroke, none of the blade sticks up into the wind. This is also used with full-length paddles. In addition to forward strokes, sliding your paddle out to an extended position adds leverage to sweep strokes, bracing, and rolling. It works with Euro paddles as well, making it one of the more useful crossover skills.

Try it slowly at first, gradually picking up the pace to your normal cadence. Either a GP or a Euro will work with this stroke, but bent-shaft paddles are awkward.

As you finish your left-hand stroke, lift the left blade from the water, slide the right hand to the middle, slide your left hand to the left, and take a stroke on the right. Repeat as necessary: slide to the middle, slide out, stroke; slide middle, slide out, stroke . . .

Sliding stroke 1: For a forward (or sweep) stroke on the right, start by sliding your right hand toward the middle of the loom as you start your wind-up. (You can slide it more for more leverage, but at first less will be easier.) PETER DONOHUE

Sliding stroke 2: Next slide your left hand out onto the left blade as you finish your wind-up, plant the right blade, and take your stroke. PETER DONOHUE

Rolling with an Extended Paddle

An extended paddle is a powerful tool for rolling with sticks or Euros and can sometimes make the difference between rolling up and going for a swim. While sometimes referred to as "cheating," anytime kayak hunters found themselves upside-down in a roll-or-drown situation, any technique that got them back upright was considered fair game. This philosophy helped them to invent over thirty different capsize-recovery techniques. You can cheat your paddle out a little or a lot, but the most powerful is the fully extended position, grabbing the end of the blade.

Roll 1: Side-by-side comparison of extended-paddle roll with stick and spoon SANDY RINTOUL

Roll 2: GPs are typically held near the end but not at the end (partly because the on-the-end grip is considered cheating in Greenland rolling competitions). SANDY RINTOUL

Roll 3: Spoons are held either at the base of the blade or at the very end for maximum leverage. SANDY RINTOUL

CHAPTER EIGHT

Safety and Rescues

Rescue Skills: Getting Started Planning to Capsize

Rescue skills, also known as *reentries* or *recoveries*, are at the core of any sea kayaker's safety net. Paddlers typically get in trouble when they end up in the water without knowing how to get back into their boats. "But I'm not *planning* to capsize" is an all-too-common refrain from inexperienced paddlers. Simply planning not to capsize is no plan at all; it's like hopping into your car without buckling up because you're not *planning* to have an accident.

Experienced paddlers, on the other hand, *plan to capsize*, thinking not in terms of if, but when. They wear their life vests and immersion gear and practice rescues regularly until they become routine. You still plan to avoid hazards, sure, but you understand that capsizing is part of kayaking, so you learn to handle it. Rather than the emotionally charged term "rescue," think of it as

Not if . . . but when ROGER SCHUMANN

a *reentry*. You've fallen out of your kayak. You don't need to be "rescued"; you just need to climb back into your boat.

Wet Exit: Getting Started Becoming a Kayaker

A key to getting totally comfortable in your kayak is getting comfortable with falling out of it. *Wet exit* (or "swim") refers to bailing out of your cockpit after tipping over. New paddlers often find the thought of being upside-down in a kayak at least a bit disconcerting, but most find the actual experience much less dramatic. (See "Wet Exit Tips for the Timid" below.) With most cockpits and loose-fitting skirts, it's common to simply fall out as the kayak tips over, but learn the proper technique, especially if you plan to graduate to snugger-fitting boats and skirts.

Before hitting the water, get comfortable releasing your skirt on dry land first, using the slap-and-slide, grab-and-punch technique.

1. **Slap.** Instead of reaching directly for the grab loop (which can be hard to locate underwater), first slap the sides of your kayak by your thighs while tucking forward. Tucking makes the grab loop easier to find.

2. **Slide.** Now slide your hands forward, following the edge of the cockpit rim or *coaming*, to find the grab loop.

3. **Grab and punch.** Grab the loop and punch forward to pull your skirt off the rim. (If you pull back, the skirt can get stuck on some cockpits, so get in the habit of punching.)

4. After the skirt is loose, run your hands back along the coaming to check that the skirt is off in back. Try it with your eyes shut while holding your breath to simulate being underwater.

5. To wet-exit for real, take a big breath and just chillax. Remind yourself that the whole process takes barely 4 or 5 seconds.

6. Flip over, either continuing to hold your breath or exhaling gently through your nose to keep water out.

7. As above, tuck forward, slap, slide, grab, and punch to release the skirt.

8. Still tucking, push the boat off of you as if slipping out of a tight pair of pants.

9. At this point your life vest will float you to the surface.

Get in the habit of grabbing your kayak and paddle as soon as you surface; in windy conditions, both can get blown quickly out of reach.

Wet Exit Tips for the Timid

- Wade out and dunk your head underwater. Falling in the water is easier when you're already wet.

- If you're feeling uneasy, have someone you trust stand beside you in waist-deep water to help you to the surface if needed; or try it first without your skirt attached.

- It's common to think you'll get trapped in the cockpit, but if you can get out easily while upright on land, you'll fall out even easier when upside-down in the water. If the cockpit feels too snug, try a larger one at first.

- Water up your nose is uncomfortable, so you might wear nose plugs or a dive mask when practicing. But practice a few times without them as well.

- Try humming. It blows a gentle stream of air that keeps water out of your nose as well as gives your mind something else to focus on. Pick a happy tune, like "Row, Row Your Boat"; you'll likely be back at the surface before reaching the first "merrily."

It's OK to capsize! PETER DONOHUE

Waiting to Exhale: Getting Serious with Controlled Wet Exits

Practice actually *hanging out* upside-down before exiting to progress to more advanced rescue techniques like the bow rescue and kayak roll.

- After capsizing, tuck your paddle in your armpit, slap the upturned hull several times, and wave your hands as if signaling for a bow rescue.

- Try counting to 10 or more before wet exiting, while slapping your palms gently against the hull in rhythm. Relax. Learn to enjoy the solitude of swaying like seaweed beneath the surface. Wear goggles and look around. If you can hold your breath for 20 seconds or more when sitting on the couch, there's no physiological reason not to be able to perform this same simple feat underwater.

- Calmly remove your skirt and slip out of the cockpit, demonstrating your control by leaving one leg in the cockpit as you surface. This leg maintains contact with the kayak while leaving your hands free to hold the paddle.

Incident Management 101

- Your first priority as a rescuer is to keep yourself safe. It never helps to create a second victim. Make sure that the swimmer isn't panicking and looking for the nearest high point to climb out of the water onto—like the top of your head.

- Make sure the group is safe so that no one else ends up in the water during the rescue. Other competent paddlers can help by picking up loose gear, setting up a towline, or watching out for less-experienced group members.

- Remain calm. Easier said than done, it helps if you practice regularly until the techniques become routine.

- Start by learning at least one assisted reentry (the T rescue) and one self-rescue technique; then expand your repertoire from there. More is better.

- Know your limits. Don't paddle in water that's rougher than you've practiced reentries in. To get a realistic understanding of your limits, train in choppy seas with more experienced paddlers backing you up.

Training Tips

For reentries to work when needed, practice regularly to keep skills sharp.

- Start in calm, shallow (even knee-deep) water to work out the rough edges of any new technique before moving to deep water.

- To train in rougher, more realistic conditions, pick a location where the wind will blow you back toward shelter, and choose your partners wisely.

- If you paddle in cold water, once you've gotten comfortable with the wet exit, you don't need to do it every time you want to practice rescues. Practice scrambling out of your boat without getting your head wet—you'll stay warmer and spend more time training.

T Rescue: Getting Started with Assisted Recoveries

At the heart of any paddler's reentry repertoire (along with some form of self-rescue) is the T rescue. Versatile and efficient, it's the go-to assisted rescue for most situations because you quickly dump the water out of the cockpit instead of slowly pumping it out.

Basic T Rescue: Bow-Up Version

Have the swimmer turn his kayak back upright so the bow is up where it's easier to grab. Remind him to *"Hold onto your kayak!"* Otherwise, wind or currents can separate boats from swimmers, requiring towlines or other more complicated interventions.

Various schools of thought about what the swimmer should do during the rescue and where he should go will be discussed below. For now, assuming he's capable, the simplest is just to leave him where he is, hanging on to the kayak by the cockpit.

1. Form a T and Lift the Bow

Grab the bow, using both hands to maneuver your kayak into the eponymous T shape. Slide the bow onto your lap.

Paddle Management: Don't let your paddle drift away while focusing on the rescue. You can slide a blade under the deck lines or bungees, but it sometimes gets tangled in rough seas. A quicker, somewhat less secure option is to tuck it across your lap, under the pouch on your tow belt, so it's slightly more secure; but keep an eye on it. Paddle leashes are super secure but create entanglement issues.

T rescue, step 1: Drag bow across deck to grab cockpit. PETER DONOHUE

2. Dump the Water: Basic Version

Before dumping the kayak, drag it across your lap until you can reach the front of the cockpit with an outstretched arm. It should now be high enough that when you flip it back upright, you won't scoop water. (If you can't get it

T rescue, step 2: Dump the water. PETER DONOHUE

that far easily, just get it as far as you can to dump it. It's more important to be fast than to get every last drop out.) See below for advanced options.

Tip: Whatever you do when dragging and flipping boats, don't be timid, especially if you're struggling at this point: Do it with *vigor*! Imagine you're wrasslin' alligators, not doing a gentle massage in water like Watsu.

3. Form the Raft

Whichever method you choose to dump the water (and more are listed below), slide the kayak back into the water, trying to angle the back of his boat toward your bow to set the next step. Lean on the bow with both hands and use it to pivot the kayaks parallel, ideally facing bow to stern (bow to bow works; it's just awkward). With any luck, the swimmer will end up on the outside of the raft, ready to crawl back in. If not, he'll be between the boats, which is the small downside to leaving him at his cockpit but isn't hard to fix.

Rather than moving the swimmer, it's faster to move his kayak. Have the swimmer grab your kayak while you pull his toward you, sliding it alongside and behind you until he's at the stern of his own boat. At that point he can transfer back to his own kayak and onto the other side as you move his kayak back into position beside you.

4. Stabilize for Reentry

To create a stable platform, lean all your weight onto your partner's kayak as if to give it a big bear hug. Either grab the deck lines nearest the cockpit on either side, or grab the cockpit coaming itself. If holding the cockpit, be careful not to block the opening with your arms, and don't let your fingers get smooshed as your partner climbs in.

Your paddle can stay wherever it is—across your lap, now forming a bridge to help further stabilize the raft, or under the bungees. Your partner's paddle can go in either place, or he can hold onto it, but it tends to get in his way if he does.

5. Reenter the Cockpit

Version 1: Belly Crawl

When you're ready, tell the swimmer to lunge across the back deck, right behind the cockpit, until his belly button is centered on the midline of the boat. Have him grab your deck with the arm nearer you to help stabilize the raft. Staying on his belly to keep his center of gravity low, he then pivots his legs into the cockpit and slides his hips back into the cockpit, without collapsing the seatback. Once his hips are past the seatback, he turns—corkscrewing

T rescue, steps 3, 4: Stabilize for reentry, belly crawl. PETER DONOHUE

toward you while still leaning on your deck for support—until his butt spins back down into the seat.

Version 2: Heel-Hook Alternative

Swimmers having trouble pulling themselves onto the back deck with their arms, a common issue, can use the heel hook to gain a boost from their legs. Facing your kayak right behind the cockpit, lift the leg toward the bow (left)

T rescue, step 5—Standard belly-crawl: Lean on rescuer's kayak and stay on belly until spinning into seat. PETER DONOHUE

T rescue, heel hook alternative for step 5, getting onto the back deck: First, hook left heel in cockpit... PETER DONOHUE

Heel hook alternative for step 5:... second, straighten left leg to lift yourself onto back deck. PETER DONOHUE

and hook your heel in the cockpit. Reach across the deck with your left arm and grab the far-side deck lines (or whatever you can). You'll be pulling yourself onto the deck with your arm, but most of the power comes from the leg in the cockpit. Simply straightening your leg helps lift you out of the water.

The heel hook puts more strain on the paddler stabilizing the kayak, so the rescuer needs to lean all her weight to prevent his kayak from tipping on its side and scooping in water along with the swimmer. (See "Scoop Rescue" below.) Once on the back deck, the swimmer can grab the rescuer's kayak to help stabilize the raft as he corkscrews into the cockpit toward the rescuer, just as described in the belly-crawl version above.

However you get him back in, continue stabilizing until he's ready to paddle. This means physically—the skirt is back on, feet are on foot braces, and paddle is in hand—as well as mentally. Check to make sure he's not too cold, tired, or freaked out to paddle on his own. If he is, a rafted tow may be necessary (see below).

T Rescue: Getting Serious

It's good to have options and backup plans. Here are a few common alternatives for dumping the water more quickly.

Edging Away

Assuming you're comfortable on edge, this trick is quicker because you only need to slide the bow onto your kayak as far as the front hatch to flip it. Then, hang on to the bow for balance while edging away until your kayak is on its side lifting his cockpit out of the water. The trickiest part is righting the kayak before you edge back upright so the cockpit doesn't scoop water. This technique is especially useful for emptying heavily laden expedition kayaks.

T rescue, step 2 alternative A: Edging away to dump water Peter Donohue

T rescue, step 2 alternative B: Elbow-curl dump PETER DONOHUE

Elbow Curl

This version is quicker but takes a bit of, um, elbow grease. Slide the kayak onto your lap only as far as the front hatch, and dump it. Reach under his bow (using the arm toward the bow) and hug his boat to your chest. Lifting the bow into the crook of your elbow, drain the kayak and spin it back upright. **Note:** Don't try this on heavily loaded kayaks or if you have back issues.

Bow-Down, Old-School Style

This oldie but goodie is handy to have in your repertoire when a kayak gets washed away from a swimmer and is floating upside-down or you're just in a hurry. Lean onto the bow with your near (right) hand for stability. Reach across with the opposite hand to lift the bow as you rock your kayak forcefully back upright, dragging the kayak, *bow down*, onto your deck, automatically draining the water as you do so. To prevent scooping water back in, use one of the options above, either edging away or using the elbow curl.

TX Version

For kayaks without rear bulkheads, water will flow with gravity into the stern when you lift the bow. You'll need to drag the kayak all the way across your lap until you reach the cockpit and can lift the stern like a teeter-totter to get the water out. A stern full of water is heavy, so the swimmer can help by pulling down on the bow as you lift the stern.

T rescue, step 1 alternative—Bow-down lift: Lean on the bow with the hand nearer to the kayak for support and lift with the far hand to drag the kayak across your lap. PETER DONOHUE

Reenter and Pump

Same as the T rescue above, without dumping the water first—starting at step 4. It could be useful if you couldn't lift the bow of a heavily loaded expedition kayak, but the cockpit will need to be pumped. This'll be twice as fast if you both pump.

Scoop Rescue

A scoop is used to rescue exhausted or injured paddlers who can't climb into their kayaks.

Scoop, step 1: Like the heel hook above, only you intentionally turn the kayak on its side to flood the cockpit in order to "scoop" an incapacitated paddler back into his boat.
Peter Donohue

Scoop, step 2: Once his leg is in the kayak, push down on the edge to roll it back upright, full of water and paddler. You then pump the water out. Peter Donohue

Assisted Rescues: Getting Serious— "Victims" vs. "Active Swimmers"

What should the swimmer do? As beginners, swimmers sometimes get called "victims" and are taught to passively cling to the rescuer's bow (so you can keep an eye on them). This makes some sense in the case of scared or novice swimmers, who sometimes do unhelpful things, like let go of their boats and paddles. But with a little training, swimmers can quickly learn to become active participants, holding on to their own gear and assisting the rescuer by flipping their kayak upright and helping stabilize the raft as they climb in.

The Role of an Active Swimmer

- Hang onto your boat and paddle.

- Participate in the recovery as a team member, while deferring to the rescuer (unless you have more experience and the rescuer requests your opinion).

- Mentality: *We're performing an assisted self-rescue to help me get myself back in my boat!*

Self-Rescue Techniques

In case whatever knocks you in the water also takes out your partner, it's best to be self-sufficient. Here are the main techniques for getting yourself back in your kayak. Ideally you'll develop a go-to method and at least one option.

Paddle Float Recovery: Getting Started with Self-Rescue

When used properly, a paddle float creates an outrigger that provides additional stability for reentry, especially for cold, tired swimmers struggling with their balance in choppy seas. A bit slower than other techniques, many paddlers find it more reliable or use it as a fall-back option. Like the T rescue, you crawl onto the back deck on your belly, then spin your butt down into the seat; but instead of a partner stabilizing your boat, you lean on your paddle float. Once back in your boat you can continue balancing on your paddle float and signal for help if it's too rough to paddle.

Besides using it for this rescue and the reenter and roll, the paddle float has several other uses. Store it someplace secure but easy to access. I stow mine behind my seat, where it's out of the sun's damaging rays, clipped with

Paddle float rescue, step 3: After attaching the float (steps 1 and 2, not pictured), lunge onto deck, hooking ankle on paddle. PETER DONOHUE

the float's attachment buckles to a strap on the back band so it's secure but easily retrievable.

1. **Attach the float.** Leaving your boat upside-down, slide a foot into the cockpit to keep your kayak from drifting away, freeing up both hands to attach the float. Slide the paddle float over your paddle blade like a pillowcase, secure it (most have plastic buckles so they won't fall off mid-rescue), and inflate it.

2. **Position your paddle.** Right your boat and move just behind the cockpit (the same place you lunge on deck for a T rescue). Form an outrigger by setting the paddle shaft in the groove behind the cockpit. Grip the paddle against the boat by slipping the fingers of your (right, in this case) hand into the cockpit and wrapping your thumb around the paddle shaft. Keep a tight grip, and keep the paddle perpendicular during the entire reentry.

    Under-Bungee Alternative: Instead of holding onto the paddle, you can try sliding the free blade under your back deck bungees, provided they are tight enough to hold it securely.

3. **Lunge onto the back deck.** As you wriggle up onto the deck, hook your (right) ankle on the shaft by the paddle float and lean some weight onto it for balance. Get your belly button all the way to the centerline, just as with the T rescue. Lift your head and arch your back to balance weight onto the outrigger.

Paddle float rescue, step 3 alternative: Using a stirrup if necessary: This out-of-water illustration shows how the swimmer steps into the loop formed by the stirrup.
Roger Schumann

Step 3 Alternative—Using a Stirrup: Trouble getting on the back deck? Try kicking your feet to the surface first, or hooking your right ankle on the paddle shaft and kicking off it.

If this doesn't work, try a *stirrup*, like on a saddle. A loop of webbing about 6 feet long is looped over the far blade, pulled down under the kayak, then wrapped up and around the shaft on your side until you have a loop hanging down that you can step into. Stirrups take extra time to rig and can create entanglement issues, but they're the only option for some.

4. **Get the first leg into the cockpit.** The key to success is to *always keep a limb and some weight leaning onto the outrigger*. Before taking your right ankle off the paddle, hook your left ankle onto it. Rotating your head toward the stern, work your right leg into the cockpit until the knee is down on the seat, keeping your left foot on the float and keeping the shaft perpendicular rather than allowing it to scissor toward the bow.

Paddle float rescue, step 4: Get first leg into cockpit, leaving left foot on float for balance.
PETER DONOHUE

5. **Get the second leg in.** Before taking your left foot off, reach your left hand onto the paddle shaft down by your knee. It helps if you move your nose over the centerline to do this. Lean onto your left hand as you work your leg into the cockpit. Keep your belly button centered.

Paddle float rescue, step 5: Get second leg into cockpit, making sure to grab shaft with left hand before taking left leg off. PETER DONOHUE

6. **Spin into the seat.** Keep leaning toward your left hand as you twist your legs around to sit in the seat. Before removing your left hand, lean on the paddle with your right, keeping weight on the outrigger. Finish with your butt in the seat, still leaning on your right hand.

Paddle float rescue, step 6: Continue to lean on the shaft with your right arm as you spin back into the seat. Peter Donohue

7. **Pump out.** Move your paddle across your lap and lean on it with your elbows for support as you pump the water out of your cockpit.

   Tip: Practice in knee-deep water to figure out the balance points before heading for deep water. Expect it to take a few attempts on either side to work out the kinks.

Reenter and Roll

This technique is performed with or without a paddle float. Basically you climb into your capsized kayak upside-down and then use your paddle to roll back up—assuming you have some familiarity with rolling.

1. To roll on the right, grab your paddle and cockpit with your left hand as you float onto your back with your feet toward the bow. The right blade should be toward the bow (with your paddle float on it, if using one). Lift your kayak onto its side as you work your feet into the cockpit as far as you can.

Reenter and roll, step 1 and 2: Crawl into the capsized kayak. PETER DONOHUE

Reenter and roll, step 3: Roll up using the paddle. PETER DONOHUE

2. Eventually you'll have to commit to reaching behind you to grab the far side of the cockpit in order to pull your butt all the way into the seat. At this point your head will go underwater as you work your legs into the thigh braces and find the foot braces.

3. Sweep your right blade out to the side as you roll up with a cockpit full of water. Anyone using this method should practice paddling around with a flooded cockpit.

Scramble/Cowboy

Successful scrambling takes a little practice, balance, and agility. But it's fast.

1. **Lunge and straddle.** Hold your paddle across the back of the cockpit as you did with the paddle float, and lunge across the deck until your navel is on the centerline. This move can be difficult without a paddle float stabilizing your kayak. If it doesn't work, it's easier to get on deck back by the hatch, or even coming in over the stern, but you'll have farther to scramble to reach the cockpit. Once your belly's on deck, spin carefully to straddle it.

Scramble, step 1: Lunge onto back deck. SANDY RINTOUL

Scramble, step 2: Scramble to cockpit, keeping feet down in the water. SANDY RINTOUL

2. **Scramble to the cockpit.** Holding the paddle, lift your chest up to rest on your elbows. Stick your feet down where the stirrups of a saddle would be to help stabilize yourself, and rotate your hips under you as if sitting "in the saddle." A common mistake that spoils a scramble faster than rotten eggs is holding your feet out behind you, as if lying on a surfboard. Keep your scramble sunny-side up by keeping your feet down the entire time.

Scoot to the cockpit on your elbows like an inchworm until your butt is clear of the seat back.

3. **Drop and brace.** Holding your paddle blade face down, ready to brace, drop your butt into the seat in one smooth, quick motion, while simultaneously slapping a high brace for balance. Turn the high brace into a sculling brace as you get your feet into the cockpit (as described for the scramble launch). Practicing these braces in calm water helps build reflexive bracing skills for rough water.

Scramble, step 3: Drop and brace. SANDY RINTOUL

Practice Tips

- Practice the different segments separately in shallow water, gradually moving deeper.

- Practice the braces in step 3 during scramble launches and landings (chapter 3).

- Paddle around on your back deck in knee-deep water to improve balance and bracing. If you start to lose your balance, simply put your feet down. When done, scoot forward to drop your butt in your seat.

- Practice balancing on your belly across the back deck in waist-deep water and spinning to straddle the kayak. Try lunging onto your back deck from chest deep, pushing off the bottom. Keep moving deeper until you can do it without touching.

Bow Rescue

Bow rescues take only seconds, because the capsized paddler never exits his cockpit. Instead he grabs the bow (or cockpit) of the rescue boat to roll back upright. It's especially useful for practicing bracing and rolls, with a partner positioned nearby.

Bow rescue 1: Safe hand position PETER DONOHUE

Bow rescue 2: Rolling up on bow PETER DONOHUE

Steps for Rescuees

Practice the Extreme Edging drill below before attempting the bow rescue.

1. **Slap and signal.** After capsizing, slap the hull to signal your partners, and wave your hands alongside your kayak. Tuck your paddle in your armpit to hold it.

2. **Maintain safe hand position.** Hold your hands perpendicular to your kayak (thumbs in) and away from the hull so they don't get smashed.

3. **Wait.** Relax—panic burns oxygen. Try hanging out for 10 or 15 seconds to give partners time to reach you.

4. **Grab the bow and roll up.** When you feel the bow, grab it and reposition it if necessary—so your palms are facing away from your face. Use the C-to-C hip snap to roll up (see below). Grab your paddle before it floats away.

Steps for Rescuers

1. **Approach at an angle.** Instead of aiming straight for his hands at 90 degrees, approach at 45 degrees, bonking into the kayak a few feet before his hands and sliding along the hull to his hands. Bonking the boat lets him know the rescue has arrived, and sliding along the hull guides your bow reliably to his hands.

2. **Be quick!** When underwater, people experience time in dog years (seven times faster than you), so don't dally.

3. **But be careful.** Use a braking rudder stroke the last few feet so you don't plow into him.

4. **If the hands disappear, STOP!** It means the person is going to either wet-exit or try to roll. Either way, he won't need your bow spearing his face as he comes up for air.

Bow Rescue Alternatives: Side by Side

If you happen to be alongside someone, grab his hand and put it on your cockpit so he can use it to roll up. Lift your knee and edge away as he pulls down so he doesn't tip you. An old-school alternative is to place your paddle across both boats and have him grab your paddle shaft to roll up.

Bow rescue, side-by-side alternative: Rolling up grabbing cockpit instead of bow
Sandy Rintoul

Extreme Edging: C-to-C Pre-Rolling Practice

This exercise isolates the extreme C-to-C motion used for bow rescues and rolling. Start by grabbing a partner's bow (or a dock) with both hands; then progress to using a paddle float and eventually to rolling up without the float.

1. Lean over and put your right cheek on your hands, holding the bow.

2. Crunch your left side into a C, letting the kayak flop over onto you as far as flexibility allows.

3. Keeping your right ear on your hands (without lifting your head), crunch into a C on the right—rocking the kayak back under you. Don't lift your head until after you've finished righting the kayak.

4. Next, lean onto the bow with your hands, but allow your head to go underwater. Eventually, let go with the right hand, letting the kayak turn completely upside-down while you're still holding on with the left hand (see top photo page 110). Then roll back upright as above. Also practice hanging out for 10 to 20 seconds before rolling up.

C-to-C steps 1 and 2: Lean onto bow. PETER DONOHUE

C-to-C step 3: Rock boat under you, head down. PETER DONOHUE

Bow Rescue Practice: Once you are comfortable with this upside-down position, hanging on with the left hand, you can move on to practice bow rescues by having a second partner paddle his bow into your right hand (if he misses, you can still roll up on the left). When you get comfortable with this, try it without holding on, waiting for your partner to reach you.

Bow rescue practice, step 1: Hold on with left hand until rescue bow reaches your right.
PETER DONOHUE

Bow rescue practice, step 2: When you grab the new (green boat) bow with your right hand, roll up on that side. PETER DONOHUE

Rolling: The Ultimate Self-Rescue

Of hundreds of rollers, I know only a handful who've taught themselves. It generally takes most kayakers a few lessons with a good instructor to learn and lots of practice to make it work in rough water. That said, get ahead of the game by practicing the bow rescue and reenter and roll with a paddle float, making sure to use good technique: leaving your head down until the very end.

Towing

Whether someone is injured or just tired, a towline can save the day. The most common tow systems attach around your waist on a quick-release belt. Being able to detach quickly if you need to is important. A good line length for flat-water towing reaches from your waist to the bow of the boat being towed, leaving about a boat length in between (around 20 feet). In following seas (with wind and waves behind you), you'll need at least 30 feet; otherwise the towed boat can end up surfing into you.

Towing Techniques

There are endless ways to tow—from simple "contact tows" using no line at all to elaborate riggings involving multiple paddlers like a team of huskies. Here are a few of the most common methods.

Getting Started: the Single-Tow Hookup

The most common and basic method is to hook your clip or carabiner to the bow toggle or deck lines of the boat you want to tow. Remember to "hook up," that is, attach the hook in an upward direction; downward hookups some-times release spontaneously when the gate hits the kayak while towing.

The hookup: Hook faces up. PETER DONOHUE

In-Line Tow

Adding a second (or third) kayak to the single tow is like adding locomotives to a train, but having more than three towers starts to get messy. Keep the strongest paddler in front, or swap out paddlers as they get tired. In-line tows are good for long distances and with rafted tows.

Rafted Tow

Use when the boat being towed needs to be stabilized because of injury or rough seas, preventing the person being towed from stabilizing himself.

Rafted tow 1: green kayak towing two orange kayaks PETER DONOHUE

Rafted tow 2: The kayaker on looker's left stabilizes the kayak of the seasick (or injured) paddler on the right, who can lie across the rescuer's kayak if necessary for further support. PETER DONOHUE

Paddle Float Tow

If there are only two of you, an unstable towee might be able to keep himself upright with a paddle float on one or both blades while you do a single tow. This can also work instead of a rafted tow if you just don't feel like towing two boats.

Paddle-float tow can work as a handy alternative to a rafted tow. Sandy Rintoul

Contact Tow

Having an unstable paddler lean on your kayak while you try to paddle is an awkward but viable option if you're alone and a paddle-float tow isn't working. Contact tows also work well for moving someone a short distance of five or ten boat lengths without bothering to deploy a towline.

Contact tow: Paddler on looker's left reaches across both kayaks to paddle while paddler on looker's right leans on his boat for support. Peter Donohue

Swimmer Tows

If a swimmer's boat blows away from him, keep an eye on the swimmer (have him hold his paddle up in the air), but go for his kayak first. It's generally easier to tow a kayak to a swimmer than the other way around. If you have help, one person can get the kayak while the other gets the swimmer. Don't expect to make fast progress dragging a swimmer.

Toggle tow: Swimmer grabs stern carry toggle or deck lines and kicks. PETER DONOHUE

Bow hug: Swimmer hugs bow as you paddle, keeping his face to side so bow doesn't smack him in the mouth. PETER DONOHUE

Back deck carry: If you have good bracing skills, the fastest way to move a swimmer is on your back deck, assuming this won't capsize you. EDUARDO SALDIAS

Section III: Planning Trips

Recife, Brazil CHRISTIAN FUCHS

CHAPTER NINE

Trip Planning: Common Hazards and Chart Reading

Taking off from land in a kayak is like taking off in a small plane—in addition to rough weather making things challenging, the farther you get from safe landing zones, the higher your levels of exposure and risk. It makes a huge difference whether you're 2 minutes or 2 hours from the nearest shelter if some nasty weather starts to blow in.

Setting out to explore Lake Tahoe KIM GRANDFIELD

Choosing a place and time to paddle that's within your skill level and the limits of your craft is the essence of trip planning. Even a basic L1 trip to the local lake to hang on the beach with your kids for the afternoon takes some planning. You won't need a compass or tide book, but you'd be wise to check the forecast for offshore winds (that could blow you out into the lake) or afternoon thunderstorms.

Sometimes planning begins with where you want to go, then layers on things like the day's weather and tidal currents to decide if today's still within your skill level. If not, approach it from the other direction: Given today's conditions, where might it be safe for me to paddle?

Common Hazards: "Know thy enemy" —Sun Tzu

Knowing what's safe implies understanding the hazards and how to avoid or handle them. The list below is elaborated upon in subsequent chapters. In-depth analyses of sea kayaker accident reports compiled in the popular *Deep Trouble* books are highly informative. Kayakers typically get into deep trouble by blundering into conditions that cause them to fall into the water without the skills to successfully reenter their kayaks. Then they drown (if not wearing a PFD), succumb eventually to hypothermia or exposure, or get lucky—being rescued via outside assistance (other boats or the Coast Guard).

- **Hypothermia:** Being immersed in water without thermal protection saps body heat at a rate twenty-five times faster than air.
- **Wind:** Blowing you where you don't want to go—like away from land—and creating waves
- **Waves/Surf:** Creating rough water that's difficult to stay upright in
- **Tidal currents:** Sweeping you where you don't want to go and creating waves
- **Headlands, rocks, shoals:** Focal points for wind, currents, waves, and rough water
- **Boat traffic:** Getting run over

Trip Planning Checklist

A key concept of trip planning—especially more ambitious trips that require calculating tides, currents, and compass bearings—is to figure out as much

Considering the next safe landing spot KIM GRANDFIELD

as you can at home beforehand rather than trying to do tricky calculations on the water and on the fly. Consider the following:

- ☐ **Chart/Map reading:** Figuring out how far and how long your trip might take, and what sort of landmarks, hazards, or areas of protection you might encounter en route

- ☐ **Considering exposure:** Gauging how friendly or how committing the shoreline is. Are there lots of easy beaches you can land on if you have a problem, or miles of wave-pounded cliffs?

- ☐ **Weather forecast:** Checking for wind speed and direction, fog, thunderstorms, etc.

- ☐ **Tides:** Checking tides and currents when applicable

- ☐ **Navigational tools and skills:** Chart, map, compass, GPS, to keep track of where you are

- ☐ **Safety gear:** Are you prepared to deal with a capsize, boat repair, injury, hypothermia? Do you have the means to contact outside help (cell phone, marine radio, etc.) if necessary? Do you have extra food, water, shelter if you get stuck somewhere?

Figuring Distance and Time: Getting Started with Trip Planning

One of the first things to know about any trip is how far it is and how long it might take. I'll often start online, using a popular mapping site for an overview and using the measuring tool to calculate distance. A screenshot of the map with the mileage marked can be printed out (see page 123). Switching to satellite view, you can glean information about the shoreline—how exposed it is, if there are landing beaches, emergency access roads or trails—and note it on the map. With this overview information, the next step is to zoom in on some details, using either a detailed nautical chart or a topographical map.

The best way to learn trip planning concepts is to plan a trip: You and your paddling partner are L2 kayakers vacationing in Lake Tahoe. A quick internet search reveals that Emerald Bay is a popular paddling destination. The map shows that the bay itself is quite sheltered, but the nearest launch site is south of the bay at Baldwin Beach. Satellite view shows that the shoreline looks rocky but landable, with only a short hike to a road if you have a problem. The weather forecast calls for light winds but afternoon thunderstorms. Drawing a route on the map, you see it's about 3 miles to Fannette Island, and your plan is to launch at 10 a.m. "Doesn't seem that far," your buddy opines. "I'm guessing we can get back before the thunderstorms start up."

Assuming you'll want to do more than "guess" with thunderstorms looming, you have a couple options. There's a formula, if you want to get serious and do the math:

Distance (in miles) / Speed (in mph) = Time (in hours)

This formula assumes that not only do you know your paddling speed but that you still remember how to do long division.

Or you can use the handy chart below. But you'll still need some idea of your paddling speed.

Estimating Time

Paddling Speed (knots)	Minutes to Cover 1 Mile
2 kts	30 min.
3 kts	20 min.
4 kts	15 min.

Estimating Paddling Speed

When planning, your speed will never be more than an educated guess, so leave in a fudge factor and guestimate low so you can be pleasantly surprised if you arrive ahead of schedule. The speeds below are commonly used for calm water with little wind or current. With practice, you'll get a better idea of your typical speed.

> 2 knots (basically 2 mph): the speed of a typical beginner or recreational kayaker
>
> 3 knots: the speed of a typical intermediate kayaker in a sea kayak
>
> 4 knots: the speed of a fast paddler

Using Knots, or Not: The *knots* used above aren't tied; they're the standard unit of speed used by mariners and equal to *one nautical mile per hour*. A nautical mile is 1.2 times a statute mile and is the standard unit used for measuring distance at sea (see below). For simplicity, you can ignore the difference and use mph for now, because your speeds aren't fast enough nor the distances long enough to make much difference.

For the 6-mile round-trip to Emerald Bay, if you paddle 2 to 3 knots, it should take 2 to 3 hours. Add another half hour or so if you plan to stop on the island:

> 2 kts = 30 minutes/mile × 6 miles = 3 hours
>
> 3 kts = 20 minutes/mile × 6 = 2 hours

Since leaving at 10 a.m. would have you returning between noon and 1 p.m., just before afternoon thunderstorms typically start, and because you have lots of landing options if things go south, you decide to go for it.

In addition to knowing the total time, it's also useful to break trips into sections by setting up a few waypoints along the route where you can get a reality check on your actual progress. For example, the halfway point to Fannette Island is near the end of Eagle Point, about 1.5 miles. Figuring out beforehand how long it should take to get there will be easier than trying to do math on the water. You'll want to know:

> If traveling at 2 to 3 knots, approximately how long should it take you to cover the 1.5 miles to Eagle Point?
>
> How long from there to the island?
>
> How long from the island back to Baldwin Beach?
>
> Answers: At 2 knots, the first mile would take 30 minutes and the 0.5 mile left to Eagle Point would take half that time (15 minutes), a total of 45 minutes.
>
> At 3 knots, 20 minutes + 10 minutes = 30 minutes.

Since each leg of this trip is conveniently broken up into 1.5-mile segments with easily recognizable landmarks (the point, the island, and back), you could expect each segment to take 30 to 45 minutes.

Keeping Track of Speed on the Water

This is all good for theoretical planning, but you also want to know actual speed. For this you'll need a watch and remember to check it at each waypoint. Knowing your actual speed can be useful for decision making along the way.

If you launch at 10 a.m. and get to Eagle Point at 10:33, you're making good progress—almost 3 knots—so you're expecting to get to the island a little after 11 a.m. If you don't arrive until 11:30, why did the next 1.5 miles take almost an hour? Were you just stopping to gawk at the stunning scenery and snap selfies, or is your friend getting tired and starting to lag behind because of a headwind blowing out from the bay after you left the protection of Eagle Point?

What if you launch at 10 a.m. but don't get to Eagle Point until almost 11 because your friend is stopping with increasing frequency to rest his arms. If it took an hour to complete the first quarter of your planned trip, your 2- to 3-hour tour is now looking like 4-plus hours; rumblings of doubt should be building in the back of your mind like thunderheads over the mountains. Instead of pushing on to the island, you wisely decide to paddle only another 5 minutes to just inside the bay to snap a few quick pics before retreating back to the launch beach.

Wind can turn this L2 trip into L3 and above, so we'll add some wind to this example in the following chapter.

Why Use Knots?

A nautical mile is a minute of latitude, so it's an actual unit of distance on your chart (and on the planet). Sixty minutes is a degree, and the Earth, being round, is divided into 360 degrees. It all adds up. The better question: Why use statute miles, an arbitrary distance of 5,280 feet?

Using Charts and Maps

Charts and maps are useful for both planning trips and for staying oriented during trips. Charts generally show more relevant details in coastal areas and lakes with a lot of recreational boating. Topographic maps are often better for more remote coastal areas, as they cover areas like inland lakes for which no charts exist. On some trips it may be handy to have both.

A chart is essentially a map for boaters, more focused on what is seen from the water with specific boater information.

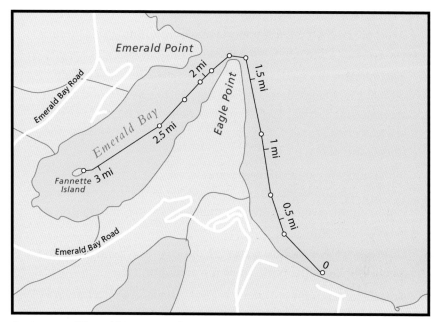

On the map of Emerald Bay, most information is land based: names of roads, campgrounds, and such. The only information about the water is that it's blue, the inlet is called Emerald Bay, and the island is Fannette.

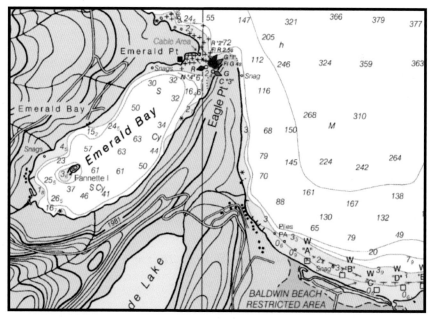

The chart gives all sorts of information useful to those on the water: location of submerged rocks, shallow water, boat channels, and landmarks visible from water level. CHART FROM NOAA's OFFICE OF COAST SURVEY

Chart Reading: Getting Started

The colors on the chart provide important information, followed by more detailed symbols, words, and numbers.

- **Tan indicates dry land,** and contour lines show how steep the shoreline is, telling boaters if there are beaches or cliffs and if there are high spots such as Eagle Point that help block the wind or low spots that funnel it. The closer together the contour lines, the steeper the slope.

- **White indicates areas of deep water** where boats don't need to worry about running aground. All the little numbers are the soundings or depth, given in meters on this chart—also commonly given in feet or fathoms.

- **Light blue shows shallow water** (on this chart, anything less than 5 meters), where larger boats could run aground.

- **Green shows mudflats** or shallow areas, usually ones that "dry" (become exposed) at low tide. In this case the green area around Eagle Point indicates a shallow area that may become exposed as the lake level drops over the summer.

- **Rocks** are indicated by crosses or asterisks, depending on whether they are submerged or awash (at or slightly above the surface, according to water levels in tidally influenced areas). Snags (submerged trees) are also indicated on this chart.

- **Boat channel** at the mouth of the bay is marked by red and green buoys, showing the deepwater passage into the bay for larger vessels that want to stay in the channel; kayaks can stay in the shallow water outside the channel to avoid boat traffic. Notice that the red buoy is on the right when entering the bay. This is always the case for ships returning to land from out at sea, thus the mariners' saying, "Red, right, returning."

View a zoomable version of the Lake Tahoe chart at charts.noaa.gov/OnLineViewer/18665.shtml. Emerald Bay is in the bottom left-hand corner.

Boat Traffic: Getting Started Avoiding Collisions

Knowing how to read charts to locate boat channels can help you stay out of them. It's like riding a bicycle on the street:

- Often you can stay on the "shoulder of the road," outside the channel.

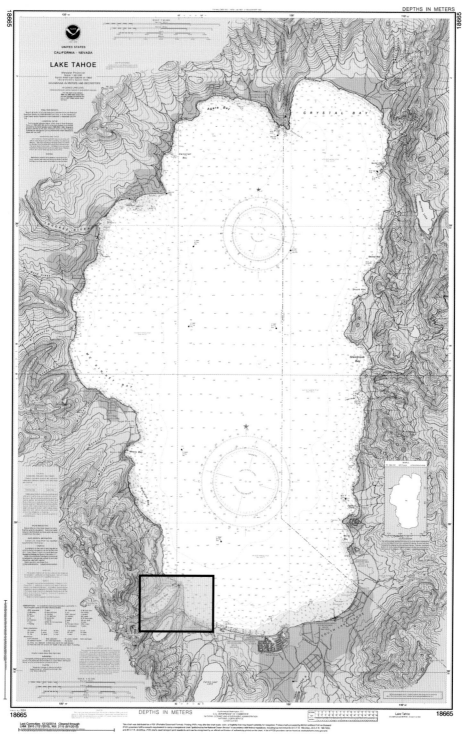

View a zoomable version of Lake Tahoe chart, with Emerald Bay at the bottom left, at charts.noaa.gov/OnLineViewer/18665.shtml. Chart from NOAA's Office of Coast Survey

Law of tonnage illustrated in extremis! SANDY RINTOUL

- When crossing a channel, look for traffic, and stay out of the way. Cross quickly, and keep your group clumped close together rather than scattered across the channel like a slalom course.
- Stay to the right when in the channel, as if driving a car.
- Rule #1: The "Law of Tonnage" states: Yield right-of-way to any vessel larger than yours.

Chart Reading: Getting Serious

Nautical charts for US waters are available online for your perusal and trip planning purposes through NOAA via an interactive, clickable map catalog with over a thousand charts cover 95,000 miles of shoreline (charts.noaa.gov/InteractiveCatalog/nrnc.shtml). You can either buy the full-size paper versions or you're free to download PDFs or cut and paste screen shots of sections you plan to paddle and print out your own, as shown below.

This chart for San Francisco Bay (opposite) is a bit more complex than the one for Lake Tahoe, as is the area it depicts. In addition to the tan, white, blue, and green areas, as on the Tahoe chart, showing land, deeper water, shallow water, and mudflats, respectively, there is some important information in purple. Dotted purple lines mark the edge of shipping channels—also marked intermittently by red and green buoys—where huge oceangoing tankers and container ships go. Shipping channels are analogous to railroad tracks on land, and kayakers should realize that large ships traveling there, like trains, won't stop or turn.

Charts have a ton of information; much of it, like the height of mid-span clearances for the Golden Gate Bridge, is only relevant to supertankers. Below are a few of the more relevant features for kayakers. NOAA's *U.S. Chart No. 1*, which lists and explains *all* the myriad symbols, abbreviations, and terms found on nautical charts, is available for free download at nauticalcharts.noaa .gov/mcd/chartno1.htm.

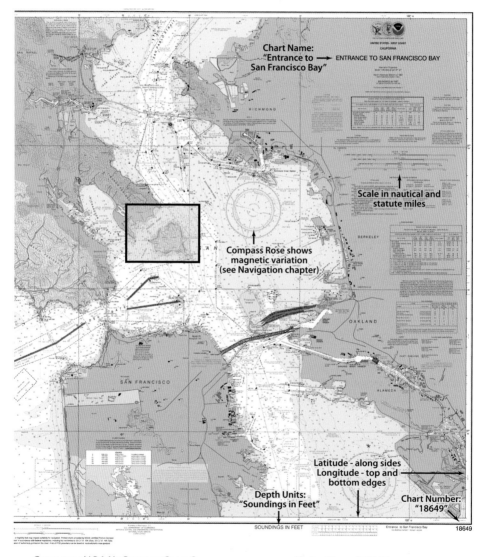

CHART FROM NOAA's OFFICE OF COAST SURVEY: CHARTS.NOAA.GOV/ONLINEVIEWER/18649.SHTML

Let's zoom in for a closer look at Angel Island, a popular paddling destination, to see what other information we can glean.

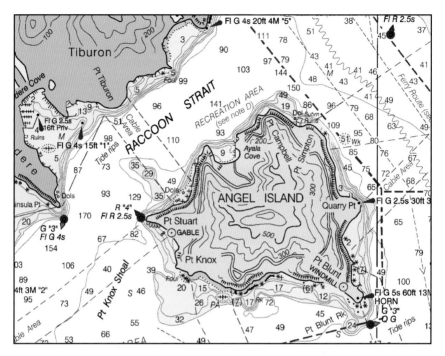

Contour lines on Angel Island (upper right), spaced at 100-foot intervals, show that the peak is 700 feet.

Pt. Stuart (far left point on Angel I.) and Pt. Blunt (bottom right on Angel I.) show a number of features.

Short vertical black lines beginning just above the letter "P" in "Pt. Stuart" and continuing up and to the right along shore depict cliffs, as do the areas above and below the words "Pt. Blunt" and several other areas around the island. Landings may not be possible in cliffy areas.

The lack of contour lines in the cove on the south side of Pt. Stuart near the "Gable," on the other hand, suggest a flatter terrain with perhaps good landing beaches in this area (which is indeed the case).

A circle with a dot in the middle indicates distinctive landmarks visible from the water and describes them. The circle just below Pt. Stuart is marked "GABLE," and on Pt. Blunt you could expect to see a "WINDMILL."

The purplish, diamond-shaped symbol in the water just off Pt. Stuart is a red buoy marking the edge of the deepwater channel. Besides the purple color indicating it is a red-colored buoy, it is also marked R "4" FL R 2.5s: R means it is red; "4" in quotes means that is the number you'd actually see on the buoy when you paddle past; FL R 2.5 s means that it flashes a red light every 2.5 seconds, which could be useful information for anyone navigating at night. Different lights exhibit different flashing patterns or "signatures" that help identify them.

The green diamond directly across the channel to the west (left) of the red number "4" buoy is a green buoy marking the other side of the deepwater channel. Larger vessels heading northeast up Raccoon Strait would go between the red and green buoys. ("Red, right, returning," remember?) This buoy, marked G "3" Fl G 4s, means it is the green #3 buoy, and it flashes a green light every 4 seconds.

Heading directly north from the red buoy off Pt. Stuart, a depth of 129 feet is shown; then there's a shoal of shallow water in blue, only 29 to 35 feet deep, that stretches halfway across Raccoon Strait. When the tide changes it can create strong currents as deep water is forced up over this shallow shoal, forming "tide rips" (areas of fast, choppy water), noted just to the left of the letter "R" in "Raccoon." Tide rips are also marked off Pt. Blunt.
CHART FROM NOAA's OFFICE OF COAST SURVEY

Latitude and Longitude

Along the right edge of the chart at left, running vertically, are the numbers 50' and 51' with prime symbols that indicate minutes of latitude. From 50' to 51' is 1 minute of latitude which equals 1 nautical mile, as discussed earlier, so many mariners will use this as their distance scale because it can be easier to find among the all the clutter on the chart than the other mileage scales.

The smaller numbers in between 50' and 51' (followed by a double prime—15", 30", 45") divide the minute into 60 seconds (60") of latitude. On the full chart you can see that the degree of latitude is given as 37°. For example, if you wanted to land at the beach by the windmill on Point Blunt, you could plug the latitude into your GPS in degrees, minutes, and seconds. Try this for practice if you want. **Note:** If you use the actual online chart, you'll see that I've cut and pasted the 50'–51' from about a mile below to fit it on this close-up; your answer will be off by a minute or so if using the example in the book. The book shows 37° 50' and about 19' or 20', which is probably close enough, as a second of latitude is just over 100 feet (101.3').

Topo Maps

Generally the most detailed topo maps available are the USGS 7.5-minute topographic quadrangles, originally a series of paper maps, now also available electronically (search "USGS Store, Map Locator" to find the incredibly long web address; or check commercial sites like MyTopo.com). As the name suggests, they cover 7.5 minutes of latitude and longitude (7.5 nautical miles from top to bottom). This series of thousands of maps covers the entire country; similar maps are available in Canada (through the Natural Resources Canada website; nrcan.gc.ca/home) and other countries.

Managing Maps and Charts on the Water

Keeping maps dry is an issue for kayakers. A waterproof chart case is a classic solution. This works well for days when you can fold your chart or map so it covers the area to be paddled until you can land and dry your hands before taking the chart out and refolding it to cover your next leg. Another solution is to copy your route in sections and laminate them in a series of pages you can put under your deck bungees and easily switch out during the day with wet hands. An economy version of this is to use gallon-size freezer bags. Along with your individual sections, having an overview map handy helps keep you oriented. For more challenging route finding, using a compass with your map may be necessary (see Navigation, chapter 12).

CHAPTER TEN

Weather, Wind, and Waves

Known as "The 3 Ws," weather, wind, and waves are three of the biggest considerations when planning and executing a trip. Unless you're paddling in remote areas off the grid, take the time to obtain a current forecast before launching—ideally a marine weather forecast if available for your area. The main thing to check is wind. An appalling number of accident reports begin with some version of "It was a calm, sunny morning, so we hadn't bothered to check the weather . . . ," only to find out after the fact that a gale was forecast.

Tony Johnson tackles L4 seas on a typical Pacific afternoon. CASS KALINSKI

Weather for Kayakers: Getting Started

For landlubbers, checking the weather typically involves seeing if it's going to be sunny or rainy and what the temperature will be so that you know whether to wear a jacket or grab a sunhat. What affects paddlers most is wind, along with the waves it can form, so wind and waves get their own categories below. Otherwise, lightning and fog are the next two biggest dangers.

Lightning

A lightning storm is a very bad place to be in a small boat. Be alert for thunderheads building. If you hear thunder or see lighting strikes, seek shelter immediately. Lightning can strike as far as 10 miles from where it's raining. "When thunder roars," goes the catch phrase, "go indoors!"

Indoors is defined as a large enclosed building, not a picnic shelter or shed. If outdoors, stay away from tall trees. Seek shelter in a grove of similar-size trees and assume the "lightning position"—sitting in a balled-up position, trying to shrink yourself into as small a target as possible. It looks a bit like praying (which might not hurt). For additional information about boating and lightning, check www.nws.noaa.gov/os/lightning/resources/lightning-safety.pdf.

Lost Coast, California BUCK JOHNSON

Fog

It's easy to get lost in the fog. Landmarks disappear; you become disoriented. If you can handrail closely along a friendly shoreline, you might be OK; but if you're paddling beyond sight of land, you could easily end up paddling in circles unless you're competent with a compass and/or a GPS. However, fog not only limits your ability to see but also can make you virtually invisible to other boats. Big boats. If crossing boat channels in fog, keep your group close together and listen carefully for approaching motors. Have your whistle and VHF radio handy, and hope those aboard can hear your frantic whistle blasts over the drone of their engines if they aren't monitoring their radios.

Wind

Wind speed and direction are a kayaker's two main considerations. A gentle breeze at your back is a great boon, but wind can be a temperamental bully at times, especially if you don't pay attention to its mood swings. Headwinds can turn a pleasure cruise into a head-down slog. Ill winds can blow you out to sea or into other hazards, like rocks, cliffs, and shipping channels. Even tailwinds can be tricky, making steering and balance a struggle if they get too strong. And all these challenges get complicated by the waves wind creates.

Knowing what to look for in a weather report—and on the water—is as much art as science. Note that wind speed is a primary defining characteristic

Finding shelter behind some rocks on a blustery day KIM GRANDFIELD

separating the various skill levels: 10 knots (12 mph) is the upper limit of L2, because that's the point when many paddlers start to struggle with steering and balance. This doesn't necessarily mean that you can't paddle anytime the forecast exceeds 10 knots; it just means that you're going to have to either out-muscle the wind or try to outsmart it, using the strategies described below.

A forecast is merely a prediction, so when you get to the beach, and especially after you get out on the water, be alert for signs that the wind is building. Whitecaps begin to form at around 10 knots (8–12 mph), making them one of the more obvious warning signs that conditions are exceeding L2 (see table below). Depending on your level, you might consider whitecaps as stop signs, alerting you to stay ashore or, if already afloat, to return directly to shore. Otherwise that easy L2 trip you'd so carefully planned can get blown into L3, L4, or even L5+ faster than you can say "williwaw."

Wind Speed and Skill Level Guide

Level	Wind Speed	Signs	Effects
L1–L2	5 kts	Light breeze, begin to feel on face, ripples and small wavelets begin to form	Minimal
L2	10 kts	Occasional whitecaps, choppy seas up to 1 ft	Begins to challenge the progress and directional control of novice paddlers
L3	10–15 kts	Frequent whitecaps, with waves and seas of 1–2 ft	Steering and progress require reasonable boat-handling skills; good balance and bracing skills helpful
L4	15–15+ kts	Frequent whitecaps, with waves and seas to 3 ft in exposed areas	Steering and progress requires strong paddling skills and the ability to edge kayak in conditions; good balance and bracing skills mandatory; some brute strength helpful
L5	15–25 kts	Constant whitecaps, spray, and occasional breaking waves; seas 3–5+ ft, exposed and chaotic	Very strong paddling skills (as above) and brute strength required

Wind direction is also important. Be particularly aware of offshore winds—wind blowing off the shore and blowing you away from it. Onshore

Launching through 4–5-foot surf SANDY RINTOUL

winds are generally safer, unless they are so strong they're blowing you out of control into something nasty, like a rocky, wave-pounded headland. On the water, pay constant attention to changes in wind strength and direction and to what you're being blown toward at any given point.

Waves

In addition to the wind pushing your kayak around, it also creates waves that roil the water and make launching, landing, maneuvering, balance, and rescues more difficult. A 10 knot wind can form 1-foot waves, both of which define the upper limits of L2 conditions. Twice the wind, 20 knots, does not simply double the size of the waves; that wind speed can form 5-foot waves (see table below) and put you squarely into L5 conditions.

For some reference points, 2-foot waves are about shoulder high to the average seated kayaker; 3-foot waves will be over your head, so when you're down in the trough, you may not be able to see paddling partners over the waves. Having buddies disappearing around like you Whack-a-Moles can be both disorienting and frightening if you're not used to it.

As the illustration on the next page shows, waves get larger the farther downwind they are blown, so it can make a huge difference whether you're paddling along the upwind shore or against the downwind shore.

How Waves Form

- Wind blowing across the water begins to ripple the surface.

- Ripples create surface area for the wind to gain purchase, so the ripples, begin to form wavelets with an even larger surface area for the wind to affect.

- Wavelets grow and form small waves—assuming there's enough time and distance over water (called fetch) for the waves to fully form.

- The stronger and longer the wind blows over open water, the bigger the waves become, eventually reaching a maximum height for that speed, duration (time), and fetch. At this point they are said to become "fully developed seas" and will get no bigger unless one of the three factors increases.

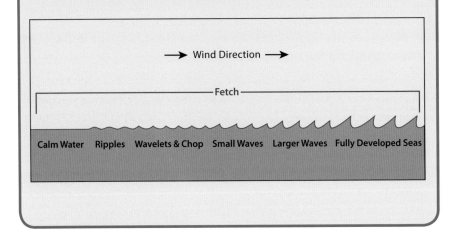

Wind Speed, Fetch, Duration Required to Form Fully Developed Seas

Wind Speed (in same direction)	Fetch (in nautical miles)	Duration	Fully Developed Seas (approx. average height)
10 kts	10 nm	2 hrs	1 ft
20 kts	70 nm	10 hrs	5 ft
30 kts	300 nm	24 hrs (1 day)	14 ft

Strategies for Paddling in Wind: Getting Started

Here are four common strategies for dealing with wind and the waves it generates.

1. **Avoid it.** Plan trips in areas sheltered from wind or on days (or times of day) with little wind forecast. Wind can be avoided by taking advantage of the fact that many areas experience a *diurnal wind pattern:* The morning starts off calm; then the wind begins blowing by midday and picks up speed as the afternoon sun heats up surrounding landmasses (hot air rising over land fuels the diurnal wind machine). As evening approaches and temperatures drop, the wind dies down. Paddle early before the wind picks up, or later when it calms down, but don't get caught out after dark without lights and night-navigation skills.

2. **Paddle in the lee.** By paddling on the leeward (sheltered downwind) side of landforms like headlands or islands that form natural wind shadows, it's often possible to paddle on days that might otherwise be too windy.

3. **Start upwind.** Instead of avoiding wind, experienced paddlers use it to their advantage. By paddling into the wind, or its forecasted direction, it'll hopefully be at your back on the return.

4. **Run downwind.** A more committing version of paddling with the wind at your back is to plan a one-way, downwind run. Two main challenges complicate this strategy. First, if the wind blows stronger than you can easily paddle against, you may be unable to return against it if you decide that you bit off a bit more than you can chew. This could commit you to continuing in dangerous conditions if paddling in areas with no road access—or worse, no landings—until your final destination, or leave you stuck someplace in the middle, unable to go back, unable to continue. Second, you need to set up a shuttle beforehand. Typically this involves leaving a car at the takeout and shuttling all the gear back to the put-in while making sure you don't leave anything behind, like your keys or your paddle, which happens with disappointing frequency.

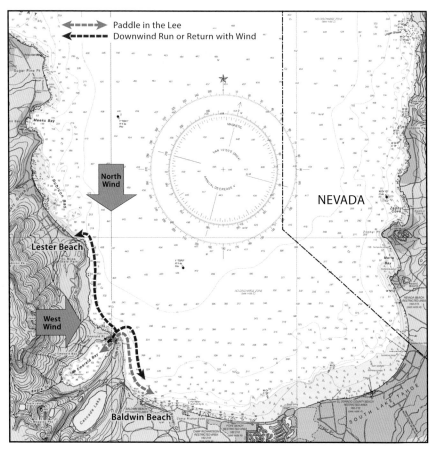

Paddle in the Lee
Downwind Run or Return with Wind

North
Wind

West
Wind

Lester Beach

Baldwin Beach

NEVADA

SOUTH LAKE TAHOE

CHART FROM NOAA'S OFFICE OF COAST SURVEY

Putting Theory into Practice: Emerald Bay Revisited

Revisiting the Emerald Bay trip, here are examples of the different strategies, depending on your skill level and the wind direction.

Tahoe Trip Example

1. **Avoid the wind.** Pick a day when less than 10 knots of wind is forecast (as in the previous chapter), or paddle early in the morning. L1–L2.

2. **Paddle in the lee.** If wind is blowing from the west or northwest, you might avoid most of it by paddling close to shore in the lee of Eagle Point. (Just be careful not to stray too far from shelter, letting the west wind blow you across the lake to Nevada.) Even with a solid L4 wind of 15–20 knots, hugging shore could keep you in L2–L3 conditions.

3. **Return with the wind.** With north or northeast winds, more experienced paddlers could paddle into the wind in the morning and return with it at their backs. **Note:** Wind from that direction could form waves on the landing beach, so having some surf-landing skills might be necessary. L2–L2+ in 10 knots of wind, depending on how big the waves get on the landing beach; L3–L4 in 10–15 knots; L4 above 15 knots.

4. **Run downwind.** An ambitious option with a north wind: Launch from Lester Beach and run with the wind to Baldwin Beach. Or with southerly winds, do the same trip in reverse, paddling north from Baldwin to Lester. Don't forget your car keys! Same levels as previous trip. The commitment level is higher, but the landing at Lester is protected because it's a north-facing beach and would have less surf.

5. **Go surfing!** Easterly winds could make for rough, wavy conditions along the West Shore—fun for kayakers who enjoy surfing, but inadvisable for those without rough-water skills and experience. L2+ in winds below 10 knots; L3–L4 in 10–15 knots.

CHAPTER ELEVEN

Tides and Currents

In some areas, checking a tide chart before you launch is as important as checking the weather. Knowing if the tide is going up or down, and which direction any associated currents are flowing, can make the difference between getting mired on a mudflat or gliding gracefully over it, and between catching a free ride on a current or struggling against it like a spawning salmon, as it sweeps you out to sea.

Reading a Tide Chart: Getting Started

While it's fascinating to understand how the moon and sun and such interact to create tides, it's more important to simply understand how to read and interpret a tide chart. Most areas have four tide changes per day, with each change taking six hours or so and the entire cycle starting about 50 minutes later each day.

On page 143 is a sample of the typical wallet-size tide books often handed out for free in coastal towns at every bait shop and convenience store. Let's look at the first line for Saturday, July 1, to see if it's a good day for a trip into the shallow channels of a coastal marsh. You want to paddle during a high or rising tide to avoid getting stuck in the mud.

There are four columns listing the time and height of each day's four tides: two low (morning and evening) and two high. (Note that this format isn't laid out in chronological order as with some books.)

Column 1 (shaded) shows a.m. low tide is at 9:20 a.m. at 0.5 feet.
Column 2 shows p.m. low at 10:05 p.m. (which isn't relevant, since you'll be home in bed).
Column 3 (shaded) shows a.m. high at 2:04 a.m. (also irrelevant).
Column 4 shows p.m. high at 4:33 p.m. This is the tide you want to catch.

High tide (top) and low tide in the mangroves, Bahia Magdalena, Mexico ROGER SCHUMANN

Three Types of Tides

There are three common variations on the theme of the daily tide cycle discussed above.

- **Semi-diurnal:** Two highs and two lows per day, approximately 6 hours apart, with the height of the highs being similar and the height of the lows being similar (common on the East Coast).

- **Mixed semi-diurnal:** Two highs and two lows per day, approximately 6 hours apart, with the heights of the highs and lows being dissimilar. Each day has a "higher-high," "lower-low," "lower-high," and "higher-low" (common on the West Coast).

- **Diurnal:** One high and one low per day, approximately 12 hours apart (common on Gulf Coast).

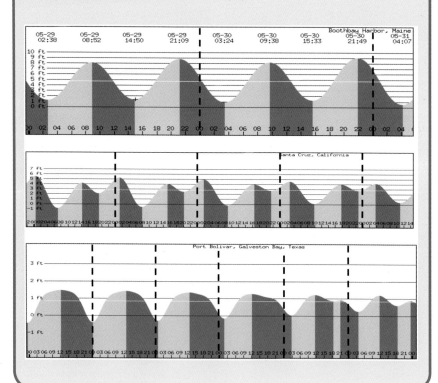

JULY 2016								
	LOW TIDE				HIGH TIDE			
	Sunrise 5:41		- PDT -				Sunset 8:27	
	AM	Ht.	PM	Ht.	AM	Ht.	PM	Ht.
1 Sa	9:20	0.5	10:05	2.7	2:04	4.3	4:33	4.2
2 Su	9:54	1.0	11.27	2.4	3:01	3.8	5:06	4.4
3 M	10:27	1.4	----	----	4:17	3.3	5:38	4.7
4 Tu	12:39	1.8	(11:03	1.9)	5:54	2.9	6:10	4.9
5 W	1:38	1.3	(11:42	2.3)	7:36	2.9	6:45	5.2
6 Th	2:26	0.6	12:29	2.6	9:02	3.0	7:21	5.5
7 F	3:09	0.1	1:19	2.8	10:05	3.2	8:01	5.8
8 Sa	3:50	-0.4	2:11	2.9	10:53	3.4	8:43	6.1
9 Su	4:30	-0.9	3:02	3.0	11:33	3.6	9:27	6.4

Assuming it's a 2- to 3-hour trip, and the afternoon sea breeze is forecast to be less than 10 knots, you plan to launch after lunch and catch the end of the rising tide.

If you want to paddle in the morning to avoid the afternoon wind, how does Sunday, July 9, look, and what time might you want to launch?

Paddling during higher tides isn't always the best choice. If exploring areas where running aground isn't a concern, you may have more landing options at lower tide. At high tide the nice little beach at the base of the sea cliffs you were planning to stop on for lunch could be totally awash.

Currents: Getting Started—Going with the Flow

The up-and-down motion of the tides can also create tidal currents, especially where the flow is constricted through bottlenecks in areas like river mouths and entrances to estuaries or between groups of islands. In this example of an estuary entrance at Elkhorn Slough, a popular California kayaking destination, tide rising on the Pacific pushes water into the wetlands. The water flooding inland creates a current called a "flood." Savvy kayakers take advantage of this current, knowing that it can boost their speed by a knot or more as they ride it up the slough. A kayaker paddling 2 knots is now going 3, with no extra effort except a few minutes of pre-trip planning.

Of course our 2-knot paddler also has to return against that knot of current, canceling out any gain unless. . . . Here are a few tricks for paddling with currents.

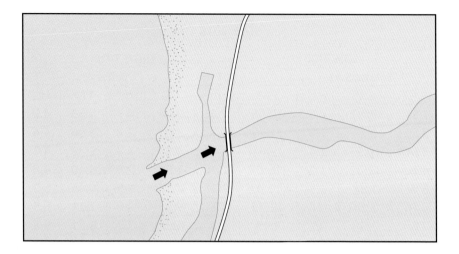

- Currents tend to be faster in deeper water mid-channel and slower next to shore due to increased friction in shallow water. A paddler returning against the flood could use this knowledge to hug the shoreline, a strategy called *eddy hopping*.

- Currents tend to be strongest at narrow constrictions, especially at entrances closer to the ocean. In this case, the gap between the jetties narrows where the sea first enters the slough, then again where the slough narrows as it passes under the highway bridge (shown on the map with arrows).

- Currents are generally faster in the middle of a tide change. For example, in a typical 6-hour tide change with a low at 6 a.m. and a high around noon, you'd expect the strongest currents between the middle two hours of 8 and 10 a.m., then gradually dissipating until 11:00 a.m., with little to no current, or "slack," for close to an hour on either side of noon.

Using this knowledge, you could paddle in with the flood tide and hug shore on your return. But a more common practice is to pick a time when you start by paddling along shore against the current (in this case, against an ebb) and riding the ebb back on the return trip, when you're more likely to be tired. With some really slick planning, you could time your trip to ride the last couple hours of the flood into the slough and then catch the beginning of the ebb current back. But as you enjoy your free ride back, don't forget that ebb currents are flushing out to sea, possibly taking you with them.

Considering Currents as Part of Overall Trip Planning: Getting Serious

Currents are just one piece of the trip planning puzzle. The wind still blows regardless of what the currents are doing. Wind blowing against current steepens the wind waves: Playful 1-foot wind waves in 10 knots of wind can double in size against 2 knots of current. Wind against current is common at mouths of rivers and estuaries, where the onshore sea breeze meets the outgoing current. This rougher water at the mouth often capsizes unwary paddlers and flushes them out to sea—a common scenario in accident reports: One minute the paddlers were enjoying a protected inland waterway, the next they were out of their boats in big, open-ocean waves.

Points of land sticking out into a tidal flow, or shallow shoals below, are other forms of constriction that can strengthen and focus currents and create rough water. If the constriction is tight enough, at around 3 or 4 knots of current, *tide rips* can form—areas of choppy, breaking waves that look like a whitewater rapid in a river.

Smaller tide rips can be a great place for L3 and L4 kayakers to build rough-water skills, especially when they are flowing into areas of calmer water where rescues and regrouping can occur after a capsize. Big tide rips are for experts only.

Surfing waves in a big tide rip, The Bitches, Wales KIM GRANDFIELD

Crossing Currents

Another issue with currents is they can take you in a direction you don't want to go faster than you can paddle. In this case you'll need strategies to cross or exit them. Use landforms such as headlands or islands that block currents, much as they block wind. When crossing currents, you can take a *ferry angle* (heading into the current to compensate for it pushing you off course) and use landforms to measure your progress to see if you are gaining or losing ground. For crossing *beam currents* (from the side up to 45 degrees) of 1 or 2 knots, estimate they'll push you about 20 degrees off course for every knot of current if you are paddling at 3 knots. You can measure this using a compass or your fist. Your fist held sideways at arm's length is about 10 degrees. To cross a 1 knot beam current, aim two fists upstream of your target. This "Quick Fist Method" is much quicker and simpler than using a compass and basically as accurate.

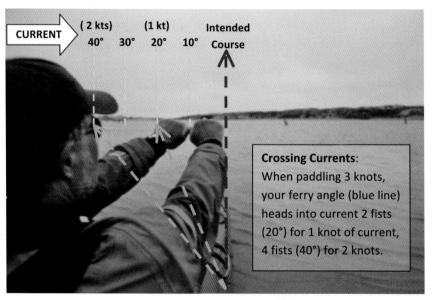

Crossing currents using the Quick Fist Method PETER DONOHUE

Information about tides and currents can be found from various sources, such as local kayak and boating stores, phone apps, and online. An excellent online resource with an interactive map of sites around the world is the University of South Carolina's "Tide and Current Predictor" found at www.tbone. biol.sc.edu/tide/.

CHAPTER TWELVE

Navigation

Navigation is said to be the art of staying found, because it's easier to keep track of where you are than to *figure out* where you are. A main key is simple awareness—paying attention to landmarks as you go and relating them to the chart.

Piloting

Piloting is a fancy term for orienting using visual references from one landmark to the next—like finding Emerald Bay from Baldwin Beach (head north along shore until you see an opening into a beautiful bay). You won't need a map, compass, or GPS to find it. You simply *handrail*, follow along a known feature (like a shoreline), until you reach a *catching feature*, an obvious landmark (like the opening to a bay, a lighthouse, etc.) that lets you know you've arrived or have gone too far.

Golden Gate Bridge at sunset KIM GRANDFIELD

Dead Reckoning: Getting More Serious

To make piloting more precise, use a chart and wristwatch to keep track of your speed and progress. Doing this when you have no visible landmarks (in heavy fog or beyond site of land) is called *dead reckoning* (from "ded" for "deduced")—estimating position based on your known course, speed, and time. For example, you're heading out of San Francisco Bay in fog so thick you can barely see the Golden Gate Bridge as you pass beneath it. To avoid the L5 conditions beyond Point Bonita, 3 miles distant, it's imperative that you recognize when you've reached it. After you paddle for a while, a point of land looms out of the fog. Is it Point Bonita already? You check your watch; only 20 minutes have passed. The currents are weak, and you normally paddle 3 knots, covering a mile in 20 minutes, so you *deduce* that you've reached Point Diablo, right on schedule. At 50 minutes from the bridge, you go on high alert. Somewhere out in the fog ahead you think you hear waves crashing. It must be Point Bonita dead ahead!

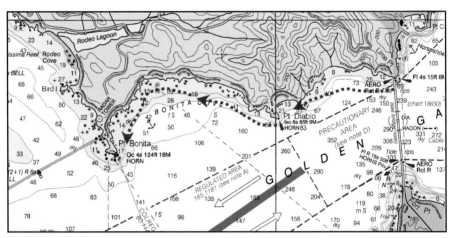

Using dead reckoning, you deduce that each of the three 1-mile sections will take 20 minutes when paddling at 3 knots, taking just under an hour to reach the dangerous conditions beyond Point Bonita. CHART FROM NOAA'S OFFICE OF COAST SURVEY

Navigating with Chart and Compass: Getting Started

Basic compass use, a core L3 skill, helps to expand your paddling horizons without getting lost in the process. At its most basic, use your compass to plot a "bailout bearing." Paddling 0.5 mile from shore you notice a fog bank blowing in. Just before losing sight of land, you shoot a quick bearing for shore, about 270°, due west. You follow the needle nervously for 10 minutes until solid land begins to dissolve out of the mists ahead.

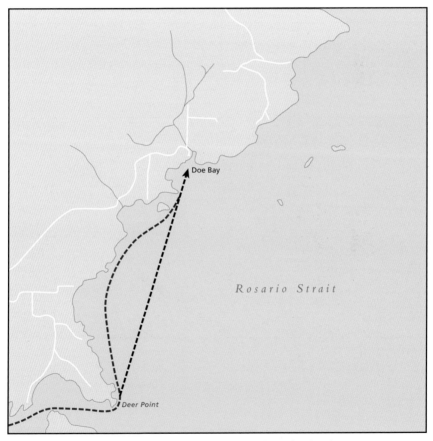

Taking a beeline directly across the bay vs. contouring along the shoreline.

A compass bearing can also help you to find things like specific beaches. In the example below, you've just rounded Deer Point and want to head straight to Doe Bay rather than take the slower route along shore. On the chart it looks easy—just head for the cove past Doe Island. But from Deer Point, Doe Island blends into the background and looks like part of the shoreline. Since you've already marked this bearing on your chart in case of fog, using the compass rose (explained below), you head due north, 000° magnetic (bearings are correctly expressed using three digits). Instead of staring at your compass the whole way, you note a distinctive saddle in the hillside at 000° and aim for that.

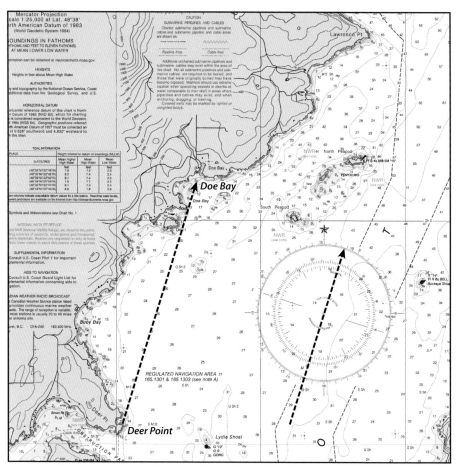

Using the compass rose to find a bearing. CHART FROM NOAA's OFFICE OF COAST SURVEY

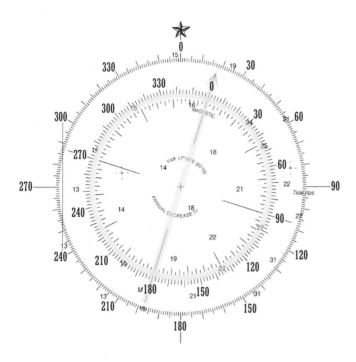

Compass rose CHART FROM NOAA's OFFICE OF COAST SURVEY

Using Compass to Navigate in Fog: Getting Serious

This same bearing could be followed in the fog using dead reckoning, but because you can't see how current or wind might be pushing you off course, it's common to *aim off*—purposely fudging to one side of your direction by about 10 degrees or so, depending on conditions. Otherwise you might hit shore, having missed Doe Bay in the fog, and you won't know if you missed to the right or the left.

In this case, aiming off to the left makes the most sense, then turning right to follow the shore to Doe Bay, rather than passing it to the right and having to backtrack. Also, if you miss it far enough to the right, you could miss shore entirely. This is where the dead reckoning comes in. Knowing the 2-mile crossing should take about 40 minutes, if you still haven't hit land in 50 minutes to an hour, you could take a sharp left turn and head 270° west, your bailout bearing to land.

Using the Compass Rose to Find Bearings

Because the compass needle points to magnetic north and maps and charts are oriented to true north, you'll have to correct for this difference. On marine charts this is easy because of the compass rose, which shows both true north (the outer circle) and magnetic north (the inner circle). The outer circle is divided into 360 degrees, starting with true north at the top at 0°. The inner circle is the same setup, only it's skewed to match the magnetic variation for the area, in this case about 17-degrees east (or right). Mariners generally use the magnetic bearing because it is the one they follow on their compasses.

Finding Magnetic Bearings: Step by Step

1. Draw a line on your chart where you want to go. This is your course.
2. Use parallel ruler to make a parallel line that runs through the little "+" sign in the center of the compass rose.
3. Read your magnetic bearing from the numbers on the inner circle (versus those on the true-north outer circle).

Tips for Making Parallel Lines

Boating stores sell *parallel rulers*. Place the edge of one ruler parallel to your course line and hold it steady as you swing the other ruler out toward the nearest compass rose on the chart (the attached arms pivot so the rulers remain parallel). Hold ruler number two steady as you slide the first ruler back next to it. Continue to slide the rulers apart and back together as you "walk" them over to the center of the compass rose, then read your bearing off the inner rose.

Two pieces of paper can be walked in the same way. Put one piece of paper on your course line, and hold it steady as you put the second piece of paper alongside it. Hold the second piece steady as you walk the first piece. Keep swapping the sheets until you reach the middle of the compass rose (see diagram).

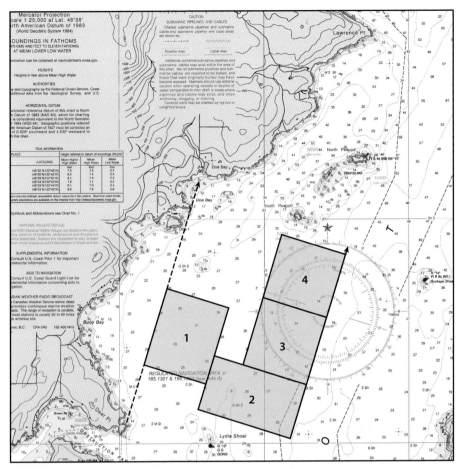

Using parallel rulers and pieces of paper to make parallel lines onto compass rose
CHART FROM NOAA'S OFFICE OF COAST SURVEY

Virtual Parallel Rulers

Word-processing programs can be used to make charts with custom bearings, as done for the illustration, although it requires modest savvy with placing graphics. Here's the step-by-step:

1. Open the chart on the NOAA website.

2. Take a screenshot (or snip) of the portion you need, and paste it into a word-processing program; crop and resize to get the best resolution.

3. Snip a compass rose from the chart, and paste it. (You may have to use the text-wrapping feature to do this. Choose the "in front of text" option, which allows you to drag the compass rose anywhere on the chart.)

4. Use the "insert" menu to draw a course line (insert > shapes > arrow). Use an arrow to show which direction you're traveling.

5. Copy and paste the course line, creating a parallel line you can then drag to the compass rose to find your bearing. Voilà! Simply print and laminate.

Bearing, Course, Heading

These terms can be a little confusing because at times they can end up being the same. **Note:** All bearings below are magnetic, taken from the inner rose.

- **Course** is your planned route, generally marked on the chart. For example, on your crossing from Deer Harbor to Doe Bay, 000°, due north would be your course, assuming no currents or wind.

- **Heading** is the actual direction you'll point your kayak to follow your course. For example, if you're taking a 20-degree ferry angle to cross a 1-knot current from right to left, your heading would need to be 020° in order to stay on your course of 000°. Without current, both your course and heading would be 000°.

- **Bearing** is the compass direction from wherever you are to some distant point. If that point happens to be your destination, then the bearing and your course might be the same. If you notice a fog bank forming, you shoot a quick bearing toward the nearest shore—270°, due west—just in case. If the fog thickens, that bearing of 270° could become your course as well. But if the fog clears and you continue on your course of 000°, then 270° is still just the bearing toward shore.

Checking the chart to find ourselves on the Lost Coast, California Buck Johnson

CHAPTER THIRTEEN

Kayak Camping

Packing for Overnight Trips

Kayak camping is like backpacking on the sea but without having to lug anything on your back. Most touring kayaks can fit a couple backpacks' worth of camping gear, allowing you to stay out for weeks if packing freeze-dried food or to camp luxuriously on short trips. On a one-nighter, a friend once pulled out a bottle of hull-chilled Chardonnay along with some charcoal briquettes and a small cooler with stuffed Cornish game hens!

Camping on a remote, no-name beach on Northern California's Lost Coast ROGER SCHUMANN

Packing tips: Use a couple duffle bags to haul all your gear—one for the front hatch and one for the rear. Lay out a tarp to keep everything from getting sandy. Pack your boat as close to the water as possible to avoid having to move a heavy, gear-laden kayak many yards to the water. PETER DONOHUE

- **Accessibility:** Keep top-priority items within arm's reach—chart, drinking water, snacks, and safety gear. Next come the top-of-the-hatch objects, such as spare warm clothes, so you can grab them quickly without having to unpack. Last are the buried-in-boat things like tents and sleeping bags that aren't needed until unpacking at camp.

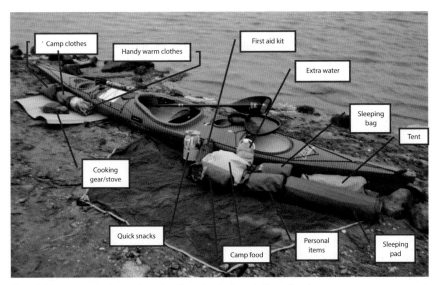

Gear laid out more or less where it will go in the kayak PETER DONOHUE

- **Balance:** Keep your boat evenly balanced side to side and front to back, but also keep the ends relatively light; this will make your boat handle better. Pack heavier items such as extra drinking water low and toward the middle; the best place is behind your seat or in the back hatch directly behind you. Because the front hatch is well forward of the balance point, your kayak will be bow heavy if you load the same weight in both hatches; 60-40 is closer to what you want.

- **Compressibility:** Cram light, skinny items you don't need quick access to—tent poles and sleeping pads—in the ends of your kayak. Then, keeping accessibility and balance in mind, shuffle the rest around like a freeform jigsaw puzzle. Avoid piling your back deck like the Beverly Hillbillies' pickup, where it'd be in the way during a rescue. If it won't fit below decks, you need to pack more carefully, get a bigger kayak, or bring less stuff.

Getting Started: Choosing Where to Go

Until you gain experience, first do some day trips in areas you're interested in trying as overnighters to familiarize yourself with the location without committing to spending the night. Consider exposure carefully: The more days you're out, the less reliable weather forecasts become. Is it possible to hike out if necessary? If not, are you prepared with extra food and water to stay put until it's safe to paddle again?

Understand that more accidents happen on Sunday than other days. Just because you'd really like to get home for work on Monday doesn't make it any safer for you to paddle in marginal conditions. A good book is an important safety item—risk-assessment experts find that people with an entertaining alternative are less likely than bored people to do something rash.

Practicing rescues with loaded kayaks is also important. Don't find out the hard way that rescuing a fully laden kayak isn't as straightforward as an empty one and that technique modifications may be needed. These are the sorts of things survivors report would have been nice to have known beforehand rather than discovering them—*Oh, by the way*—with their lives on the line.

As you gain skills and experience, you'll find your horizons expanding, stroke by stroke, drawing you onward toward whatever adventures await, big or small. Enjoy the journey.

Seeking shade, Sea of Cortez, Baja California, Mexico ROGER SCHUMANN

Index

About the Author

Roger Schumann is the founder and primary instructor for Eskape Sea Kayaking school in Santa Cruz, California. Winner of a National Outdoor Book Award, he's the coauthor of *Sea Kayak Rescue* and *Sea Kayaking Central and Northern California*, a contributing writer to *More Deep Trouble,* and the author of numerous magazine articles. He's been teaching sea kayaking for more than twenty years as an ACA-certified, Level 5 instructor-trainer; he's also a member of the ACA's Coastal Kayaking Committee, an instructor-trainer for surf kayaking and SUP, and a whitewater kayaking instructor. In addition to the California coast, a few of his favorite paddling destinations include Alaska, North Carolina, Baja California, Argentina, Brazil, Belize, Chile, Canada, Scotland, the Apostle Islands, Lake Superior, Deception Pass, Washington; Green River, Utah; and Grand Canyon, Arizona.